Comments from Readers:

"The encouraging message in *God's Heavenly Answers* must be read by those who are struggling in the darkness of despair and sorrow. It is rich in wisdom and practical answers for all. This book is a self-contained support group!"
  Kevin A. Brown, Attorney at Law

"I want to thank Joyce Brown for putting things back in perspective for me. The day after I read this book (I read it in one sitting!), I viewed my life from a completely different, and much improved perspective. It's great to be reminded in such a compelling way about what really matters most—now and in eternity."
  Janice Kapp Perry, Author, Composer

"I've known Joyce Brown since before the events she describes in her book . . . I was aware of a marked change in her approach to life afterward. She now handles difficulties and challenges with the confident attitude of one who has the peace of mind that comes from knowing her purpose and direction in life. Her story will greatly enrich the life of anyone who reads it."
  S. Burt Chamberlain, MSW, Ed.D.

"I have read everything I could find on near-death experiences for the last 32 years. This topic of what happens on the Other Side of our existence is very important, comforting, uplifting and interesting. It also gives knowledge of what's ahead of us. This book has all the answers to all the questions anyone will ever ask about what happens when one passes over to the Other Side of existence. Information contained in this book really gives answers to the reason why we are here and in this place. It tells us what consequences we face for our actions and what we should be thinking about and how we should live our lives every day. I recommend this as required reading for everyone!"
  Devin Thomas

"Thanks, Joyce, for writing this book. It is one of the most powerful and life-changing books I have ever read. It has given me a new understanding of life and how to enjoy the Other Side when I get there."
  Jim Robbins (Jim's quote after reading a previous edition just shortly before he passed. Jim is Tony Robbins' father.)

D0359486

"About 5 years ago, I was blessed to meet Joyce Brown. She had given me her book (*God's Heavenly Answers*) to read. I was going through a lot at that time and I was addicted to drugs. I started reading the book, but ended up in jail before I could finish it. Joyce visited me in jail and arranged for me to receive another book so I could finish it, which I did while in custody. I can't tell you the power that book had in my life. I didn't get clean from drugs right away, but that book gave me hope and I no longer wanted to die. Now, I am 16 months clean and sober and am undergoing treatment for Hepatitis C. Some days are really rough and seem almost unbearable. But I make it through the day with the hope Joyce shares in her book. I believe in the message the book sends out to all those who are having a hard time in life. I encourage you to read her book. It had a life-changing effect on my life. I just want to say thank you, Joyce, for having the courage to write this book. It has helped me immensely. I will always have a special place in my heart for you. Thank you."

Barbara Cimino, Former drug addict

"Thank you for writing your book. It gave me a different perspective about life and my problems. Now I have found reasons why I want to live instead of automatically wishing I could die or wanting to trade places with someone else."

Michelle L, Student, Age 14

God's Heavenly Answers

~

Near-Death Experience Revealed

How to Make Certain You Enjoy the
Other Side When You Get There
with **Stress and Grief Relief Now**

A True Story by

Joyce H. Brown, Ph.D., ND, EFT
Foreword by Kimberly Clark Sharp, MSW
Author of After the Light

✳ DAVIDSON PRESS

Stress and Grief Relief, Inc., 450 Hillside Dr., A224, Mesquite, NV 89027
Phone: 1-800-675-1777 • Email: askwisdom@yahoo.com
Website: StressandGriefRelief.org

God's Heavenly Answers™
New Edition

Copyright © 2014 by Joyce H. Brown. All rights reserved.

No part of this publication may be reproduced in any form or by any
electronic or mechanical means, including information storage and
retrieval systems, without written permission from the author, except
by a reviewer, who may quote brief passages in a review.

10   9   8   7   6   5

Printed in the United States of America

ISBN 978-0-9913320-2-1 (Paperback)
ISBN 978-0-9913320-3-8 (E-Book)

Note: This book is not intended to replace the advice or care of
professional health-care practitioners.

✳ DAVIDSON PRESS

450 Hillside Drive, A224
Mesquite, NV 89027
1-800-675-1777 or 1-626-791-1211
Email: askwisdom@yahoo.com
Website: www.StressandGriefRelief.org

Lovingly dedicated:

To my family, friends, and associates who have encouraged me, cried with me, laughed with me, and endured my times of learning.

To anyone along the way I may have offended as I was growing wiser and learning . . . I apologize.

To all those who believed in me and cheered me on when things seemed darkest.

To all those who have succeeded in life leaving an easier path for others—including me—to follow.

To all those who have entrusted me to be their mental cheerleader.

To my ancestors and posterity, my Other Side's cheerleaders.

To all those who have a desire to know more of the Other Side, to live life to its fullest, to not only find a better way, but to help create a better way of living and learning from and with each other.

To those who endure and REAP LASTING PEACE OF MIND!

The profits personally realized by the author from the sales of this book are donated to Stress and Grief Relief, Inc., a 501 (c) (3) nonprofit organization for the purpose of sharing this book's message of God's Heavenly Answers and for the prevention of depression and suicide.

For more information visit:
www.StressandGriefRelief.org

or call the Suicide Hotline:
1-800-675-1777

Acknowledgments

AFTER I WROTE THE first draft of this book, the encouragement I received from family, friends, readers, and those who helped me get it published was heartwarming and miraculous.

When God brought certain people into my life, with them came miraculous answers to prayers and treasured blessings. Words are inadequate for me to thank many of them for their care and concern. However, I want to express love, gratitude, and appreciation to all who have encouraged me and so willingly assisted in making a new edition reality.

Not all can be named, and my list is growing, because so many are helping me make this new edition possible. So many I want to thank who have been part of my story, and have encouraged me along the way. I love and appreciate them all. However, I will attempt to name only a few of those whose circle of love and prayers have assisted me tremendously.

First, Ron, my loving and caring husband, my mother, Viola, who is now deceased, and my three grown children, Suzan, Patty, and David. Many other loving family members I won't try to name, including step-children, grandchildren, and great-grandchildren.

Also included in this circle of loving support are special friends whose efforts and help made this new edition possible; such as LeRene, Gregg Christoffersen, Dave Hodgson, Esq., Robin, John, Jim and Fern, R. T.; Bob and Carol, Lorina Novasio, June Davidson, CSL, MCAC; Cathy Carroll; John Welch; Tina Foster, writer/author/editor; Kare Neve, and Duane Kendall, web master; and Jayson Hamilton for his computer genius as he rescued me from crashed computers.

Dr. Hiten Shah for his life-saving care and advice for me and my husband, Ron.

A great thanks to Bill Sardi, investigative medical reporter and author of 12 unique books on health that offer information not available anywhere else. I thank him for the miraculous recovery of my vision, twice from severe macular degeneration. I would have no vision at all without Sardi and his product Longevinex™. My story won an Emmy Award as reported by George Knapp on CBS 8 News Now.

Thanks to George Knapp's reporting; it has given me the opportunity to share the message of my vision recovery so others were able to gain their vision as well.

A very special thanks to Gary and Joy Lundberg, authors of several books including *I Don't Have to Make Everything All Better.* Their willingness to share their personal knowledge and give guidance has been priceless. Special appreciation is also expressed to Kimberly Clark Sharp, author of After the Light, who wrote the foreword. Arvin Gibson, author of several books of people's Near-Death Experiences on the Other Side, including Echoes from Eternity, Glimpses from Eternity. RaNelle Wallace, author of *The Burning Within*; Warren Jamison, author of top-selling books, was a great supporter.

Special acknowledgment to Roger Magnuson Esq., one of the top 500 trial lawyers in the U.S. He was my personal attorney for five years of my devastating environmental business lawsuit that I was legally forced to go through. Afterwards, Roger was a great friend and encourager as I changed direction of my life from environmental health and alternative fuels to focusing on sharing *Heavenly Answers.*

Special appreciation is also expressed to Lee and Joyce Saunders. A special thanks to Robert Davis, for his input and skills. Another special acknowledgment and thanks to Darla Isackson, author of *Finding Hope While Grieving Suicide* and other books. Her editing, insights, talents, and inspired suggestions have been priceless. Darla's unique editing talent helps authors write what they mean to say, and to keep on keeping on until their manuscripts are complete.

A special, special thanks to David and Edna Allan whose prayers and words of encouragement have strengthened me, and now made the hope of this new edition an actual reality. David is an internationally renowned Atomic Clock Physicist and author of *It's About Time: Science Harmonizes With Religion.* Edna is a talented, loving friend and wonderfully gracious and elect lady. Again, words are inadequate for me to thank them and their family, except to say that they truly are Earth Angels.

I would like to thank the readers who have brightened many of my days when they wrote to me with their comments and their stories of the book's life-changing effects for them. Also, I have received letters and calls from numerous people who have let me know that they changed their minds about committing suicide after reading this book. Hearing from my readers is like receiving a gift that helps me continue with my life's journey and mission to share the heavenly answers and messages that were revealed to me while I was on the Other Side.

An extra special thanks to Nick Zelinger, a talented, patient, and award winning graphic designer. I encountered unexpected delays in getting my book published. Miraculously, I found Nick. I had to re-title the book to *God's Heavenly Answers* and republish it. Nick redesigned the cover, typeset the interior with updated changes, and prepared the files for publishing. He did a fantastic job. I am very grateful.

Jim Quick, a brilliant, knowledgeable, and very experienced Enrolled Agent, who helped me create the non-profit Grief Relief Now, Inc., in 1999. Since then he kept us on track and has become more than a good friend. He is like family and a great supporter.

Melissa Welles-Murphy. Many thanks for your personal encouragement. You have done so much for so many of us in our quest to enlighten the world about natural health and it's many modalities.

Special recognition and appreciation for the International Association of Near-Death Studies (IANDS) and their supporters. Their dedication to the subject and their hard work make it possible for those of us who have had NDE's to share our stories with the world.

For more information, visit my website at:
www.StressandGriefRelief.org

Email me at: askwisdom@yahoo.com

Foreword

by Kimberly Clark Sharp, MSW, Author of
After the Light

FOR ANYONE WHO HAS ever toyed with the notion of "ending it all" in an attempt to go to the place of love and light, Joyce Brown offers an important reality check. There is a *reason* why we are here and why our life is not over, no matter how bleak our current situation may be. Immense rewards—spiritual rewards—await those of us who persevere in the face of trials and try our best to learn and to grow.

In my own book, I wrote: "The Light was brighter than hundreds of suns but did not hurt my eyes. I immediately understood it was entirely composed of love, all directed at me. I was with my Creator, God, in holy communication. The Light gave me knowledge that I seemed to be remembering rather than learning, and included answers to questions that any fool would ask in the presence of the Almighty. 'Why are we here?' *To learn.* 'What's the purpose of our life?' *To love.* And, among other questions, 'What about suicide?' The answer I understood was, *'If you didn't create it, you can't destroy it.'* I took that as advice to not deliberately end our earthly lives prematurely. Why not? Well, if life is a metaphor for school, consider that if we drop out in say, March, we cannot at such time as we figure out we need more education, begin again in March. We have to repeat the entire school year and probably have to take remedial classes. We end up working harder than if we had stuck it out in the first place."

I wish I had been able to convince Joyce Brown of this earlier in her life, but then she would have missed the most remarkable experience of her life.

After a prolonged and serious illness with debilitating pain, Joyce Brown willed herself dead. She had a near-death experience, but it was not what she expected. Instead of bliss and blessedness, she had an "extremely anguishing experience" wherein she suddenly realized all that she had lost by giving up on life. The wispy spiritual body she now possessed could not speak to her loved ones or pick up pen and paper to write them. She was overwhelmed by a desperate longing for her pain-racked earthly body as she realized that she could no longer communicate to her family how much she loved and missed them. She had her chance at earthly life and now it was over.

But fortunately for us, it wasn't over. A "beautiful Being of Light" ushered her into His presence and began to teach her about life. She saw that life is like a race and that it is important to continue that race until its natural end. The barriers and obstacles that we encounter on this race are there to help us learn and grow.

She was shown the agonies of people who had ended their lives early and who then tried desperately and without success to warn others who were present at their funerals. She came to know that there is no such thing as "ending it all" and that the problems people face may even get worse when they terminate their lives before their time.

She learned how people who appear to "have it all" really don't and why we would not want to trade places with those who seem to float through life unscathed by problems. She was taught why we have the problems we do and how we can learn from every situation, no matter how difficult.

Then she saw that rich rewards and priceless joys await many of the most humble people on earth who valiantly suffer through their trials and tribulation. Fortunately for whiners such as myself, complaining while suffering is okay.

She witnessed intense marital arguments from inside the mind of each participant and could see that what they were saying did not correspond with how they were really feeling. She saw the utter futility of bitter, heated disputes and learned how such conflicts could be resolved. She also saw a miserable place for souls who died while still holding onto their spiteful grudges.

Accordingly, Joyce came to understand that any deed we do with unrighteous motivation or intention actually hurts ourselves. On the other hand, forgiveness—whether requested or not, whether deserved or not—brings heavenly rewards beyond comprehension.

In summation, the things we say and do on earth can drain or build our character and spiritual strength with results that show up when we arrive on the Other Side. The way Joyce figures it, we are literally building a heavenly retirement fund!

When confronted with the question, "In life, what did you do with what you had?" none of the carefully crafted excuses that had previously shielded Joyce from accepting responsibility for who she was and how she acted had any effect. In re-experiencing everything that happened in her life, she realized we "score" simply by how well we do with what we have.

She learned that miracles are actually common and happen more easily for those who believe in them. She was surprised that more of her prayers had been answered than she realized and that she had been blessed many times without knowing it. She also saw the difference in how beauty is created and valued on earth and how beauty is created and valued on the Other Side. Her insights reinforce the timeless truths from Jesus' Sermon on the Mount.

Joyce Brown asks us to please hear her message: *Life is Worth Living!* I agree with my whole heart. There is a peace in knowing that a great leveling is coming, that every valley shall be exalted and every mountain and hill made low, that people who lead lives of challenge and heartache have greater growth opportunities than those who have lives of ease; that this is our chance to learn and grow spiritually, to experience and accomplish things that can only take place in an earthly existence.

We get up from reading this book grateful to be alive and to have the chance afforded by each day to do good and to be good. There is power in the lessons of this book, power that the least of us can use in meeting the challenges that come to us every day.

This book is about life and afterlife. It helps us understand the big picture—why we are here and why life unfolds as it does—and it helps us gain strength for the daily challenges we all face as long as we exist in earthly form. Life indeed is worth living and *Heavenly Answers for Earthly Challenges* helps us understand our personal purpose and path.

Contents

Part Four
My Life after I Returned to Earth

PART ONE

~

Myths vs.
the Reality
of the
Afterlife

Chapter 1

≈

Why I Had to Write This Book

RECENTLY, I WAS VERY ill and there were several days when I wondered if I would be called to the Other Side—this time for good. That thought greatly worried me; I did not want to die before I finished what I was supposed to do on earth. I knew that more was expected from me because of what I had been shown when I had a near-death experience and was on the Other Side. I had not yet shared this experience with some special loved ones and others because I was worried about finding the right words and what their reactions would be.

Fear Ye Man More than God?

A Whispering of the Spirit

Being so ill, and completely losing my voice for over two months kindled my fears that I might never be able to share my experience. A soft whispering of the Spirit came to me with a question that seemed to ask, "What is your priority now? If you could, would you speak up? Fear ye man more than God?" I came to the point that all I could think about was recording my experience; I began working on it immediately.

If I can help anyone realize the importance of living life in a way that can help them achieve a portion of the joy and peace of mind available on the Other Side, I must do it. I want peace of mind the next time I die. When I am questioned again as to what I did with what I had, I hope I can say that I helped many others with the knowledge I was given.

Myths of the Other Side

"Let me out of here . . . I want to die!"

Those words expressed my feelings from the time I was a small child. If I had been asked whether I wanted to live or die, the truthful answer usually would have been, "I want to die."

From my youth, I remember hearing how nice it was on the Other Side and how happy people were after they died and left this earthly existence. Life after death sounded appealing to me.

However, in January, 1983, when I was 49 years old, I had an experience that forever changed my view about committing suicide or even voluntarily giving up and choosing to die. It involved my own long-desired death and a glimpse of the life beyond. Some people call such events near-death experiences and they are talked about more openly now than in the past, for which I am grateful. This openness helped me have the courage to share my experience on the Other Side.

During my near-death experience I discovered that the imagination can falsely influence someone into thinking that killing oneself will take him or her to a better place than this world. It's true that a glorious, peaceful sphere may await us after we die. *Suicide, however, will not put us there!*

Now I see life, death, and life after life from the position of a person who sincerely desired to die and now places a great value on life. Also, I know that life is precious beyond all comprehension and that our time here is too precious to waste.

The Race of Life

While on the Other Side, I saw that life is similar to a race that starts at birth, and that when I was on earth I was one of the participants. I saw scenes of a race, and I was running with other runners along a designated course. Then thoughts came to my mind: what if somewhere in the course of the race, I decided I couldn't wait to get to the finish line? Maybe I was too tired to go on, or I felt the race was harder than I had anticipated. Would this justify my cutting across the field, running directly to the finish line, crossing it, then expecting to claim the rewards of a great victory?

What would I really have accomplished? Even if I might fool those who didn't see me cheat, did I think I could fool the judges? Did I think they might conveniently be looking away at the exact moment I took the shortcut? Or could I console myself with the wish that they loved me so much they would forgive me—that no consequences would flow from my fraudulent action?

Did I think I could be considered a winner if I didn't *earn* the victory? I knew it would be an empty victory, and in reality, a defeat. Even if the judges forgave me, I would still know. How long would I carry my guilt and shame before I would be able to forgive myself? Lastly, what of the others who witnessed my cheating, and were influenced to also take the shortcut? Would I not hold a part of their guilt as well? I recognized that taking a shortcut in a race is symbolic of suicide.

No Competition

On the Other Side, I discovered that life is precious and only if I explored it to its natural conclusion, could I have the peace of mind and victory I hoped to claim. Also, knowledge was given me that during my time on earth, I was not competing with anyone but myself. I knew that the only approval I really needed was from that Great, Loving, all-knowing Being, the Creator of the Universe—and from within myself.

My Father's Near-Death Experience

I've heard accounts of individuals who have had near-death experiences who tell of their wonderful feelings of peace. It so affects them that they are powerful witnesses of the beauty of the Other Side. Sometimes others who are troubled hear these stories and become convinced that they could find that love and peace if only they could die. I believed that!

When I was in my teens, my father told me of the near-death experience he had when he was seriously injured in a car accident in the early 1950s. He told me of the beauty of the Other Side. This encouraged and reinforced my tendency to see death as an escape from my problems on earth rather than to seek for answers and solutions.

The near-death experience that my father had, I believe, had a tremendous effect on him, too. Later, in July of 1980 when life apparently seemed overwhelming to him, he committed suicide. I had not heard from him for some time before I received the phone call telling me of his death.

At the grave-side services for my dad, I sat staring at his steel-gray coffin. The atmosphere felt dark and heavy to me. It was as if I could feel some of the despair he felt before he took his life. I foolishly thought about joining him in death, not realizing that suicide would lead me to anguish rather than peace.

My father's death by suicide is not something I have generally made known. The decision to mention it here follows deep soul searching. The last thing I want to do is hurt those close to me—members of my family who did not know. Suicide is a subject usually not discussed. His suicide was sad, but it happened, and it added to my misguided thoughts that suicide was a positive alternative.

Because of What I Know, I Must Speak Up

Because of the fear that I might hurt someone's feelings, I was reluctant at first to speak up. I would not want to cause pain to anyone who has lost a loved one to suicide. Yet, I know that there are innumerable people who mistakenly feel as I did when I believed that all I would have to do is give up and die or commit suicide to find lasting happiness. I feel compelled to share what I experienced and what I personally learned on the Other Side in the hope it will save lives and needless anguish for many.

When I was on the Other Side, I gained a new perspective from what I was shown and what I learned from glimpses of premortal life. Scenes of the spirit world, including revelations of knowledge were impressed upon my consciousness. When viewed from the perspective of life in the hereafter everything fits together perfectly. Because of what I learned there, the real purpose for living and making right decisions became clear—as did the reasons not to give up when tempted to do so.

Chapter 2

~

Anonymous and Comfortable

A FEW YEARS AGO while deep in thought, I suddenly became aware of the midday news that was on television. The anchorman was discussing specific near-death experiences that people had related to him. Even with the differences in their stories, there were those words again! They were saying that it was so peaceful and beautiful on the Other Side that they hadn't wanted to come back.

Since my own journey to the Other Side, those descriptive words have lost their attraction. Instead, they now fill me with great remorse. Many feelings welled up within me as I remembered my own experiences over there.

I wanted to cry out, "Please, you are telling how it is only for those who are ready to meet their Creator and who do not voluntarily take their own lives."

Silently staring at the television screen, I sat there thinking and reliving some of my own experiences. Then I heard a news item from a second reporter about two teens' suicides. A boy and a girl left a note saying that they had entered into a "love pact" before killing themselves. They did this mistakenly believing they would leave this earthly life to go to a more beautiful place where they would happily be together forever.

Earlier that week, a seventeen-year-old, who seemingly had everything to live for, killed himself. He came from a well-respected family and was active in his religion and sports. He was admired in many ways and held a leadership position at school. From outward appearances he was truly living the American dream.

Many thoughts went through my mind as I heard the news commentator speculating on the cause of his suicide. Too much stress at school? Too much peer pressure? An investigation was in progress to determine whether the three dead teens had known each other. Were there connecting factors, or should their deaths be categorized as unexplained "chain suicides?"

As I listened to the newscaster stating possible reasons for those young people killing themselves, I shuddered. I was literally quivering as I went to the television set and answered it as if I could be heard. "No! No! Those are not the reasons those teens killed themselves." My mind flashed back to some of the things I had seen in my near-death experience, especially about teen-age suicides. I felt I had to warn the newscasters of the dangers in unequivocally using phrases such as "how beautiful and peaceful it is on the Other Side."

False Beliefs Can Lead to Tragedy

Falsely believing that in death they will find relief from all worldly cares can be a powerful enticement for those who feel overwhelmed to kill themselves—especially troubled young people. I know of such feelings from personal experience!

After the news broadcast was over, I sat on the couch wondering what I could do that might make a difference. Feeling compelled to speak up, to do *something*, I realized I could do it in a safe way as I dialed the phone number for the television station.

A woman answered with the call letters of the station. My voice was trembling, but I expressed my feelings about the dangers of the words used by the newscaster. After a pause she said, "Just a moment, please," and put me on hold. I wanted to hang up, but the security of being distanced by the telephone, of being a nameless, faceless person just telling the station my opinion, gave me the courage to hold on.

The Other Side Is Not Always Nice

After a time, a man's voice came on the line. "Can I help you?" he asked. With a jolt I recognized the voice of the anchorman himself, the one who had reported the teen-age suicides. My nervousness began to disappear as I explained the possible danger in how teenagers and others *could* perceive his program's message.

"It's not always beautiful for someone on the Other Side," I went on in fervent tones. "The Other Side is not a place to escape problems. It is only peaceful over there if the timing is right and we do not give up on life. When someone gives up and commits suicide, they may discover on the Other Side that there were answers available for them *on earth* for their problems. This may cause them to feel tremendous anguish and it can be terrible for them over there."

How Do I Know? I've Been There!

His quick reply caught me totally off guard. "How do you know?" It seemed as if the telephone receiver were made of lead. I didn't feel like a nameless, faceless person anymore, but I also knew I had to truthfully answer his question. Up until this moment, I had only shared my experiences on the Other Side with those few I had felt comfortable telling about the matter. Now, all previous reluctance to speak felt like something tangible that surrounded me.

"Because I've been there," I answered with calm assurance. I felt as though I were standing in a public arena making my announcement to the whole world. If he asked me, I knew I would have to meet with him personally, speak up, answer his questions, and tell him what I had experienced. This would mean leaving my comfortable, anonymous position to substantiate the statements I had made. However, I was ready—even for interrogation if necessary.

My thoughts seemed to hang in the air as I waited for his response. . . . Silence! At last, he asked for confirmation in a softer, more open tone, "You have been to the Other Side and back personally?"

When I assured him that I had, he continued, "What you experienced over there makes you believe that there's a connection between these teenage suicides and our television coverage of people's stories about how happy they were on the Other Side and how beautiful it was? Is that correct?"

"Yes. Most definitely, yes," I answered quickly. "Even if there's only a remote possibility that your broadcasts were a contributing cause and were glamorizing suicide, can you afford to take the chance?"

This time he didn't hesitate, but concluded in a friendly tone. "My co-anchor on the show has been concerned about this himself. We'll take the matter under advisement here at the station. Thank you for calling." With that he hung up.

Lasting Peace

Oh, what a relief. I was back to my comfortable, anonymous position even though I had not backed away from his questions. He had listened politely, and I felt I had accomplished something by communicating at least a tiny part of what I had experienced on the Other Side. One reason I had wanted to come back to this life was to warn others and to share how to find real joy and peace of mind over there . . . *lasting peace.*

Later that day, I found out that the televised newscast I had seen that prompted my call was the third in what was to be a five-part series for the week, and each aired both morning and evening.

Self-Deluding "Love Pact"

The seventeen-year-old boy had killed himself within hours of the first evening's broadcast. The boy and girl who had made a self-deluding "love-pact" killed themselves within hours of the second evening's broadcast. This, the third, was scheduled to be rebroadcast on the evening news. Five more broadcasts were scheduled.

Fearing the effect the broadcasts could have, I wondered if what I had said could make any difference. Sitting down again on the couch, I leaned back, closed my eyes, and waited anxiously for the program to come on.

Finally, it was time for the broadcast. As I watched, I was pleased to find that telling the news commentator some of my experiences from being on the Other Side *did* make a difference—the remaining broadcasts "glamorizing" the teens' chain-suicides were canceled.

No Such Thing As "Ending It All"

Suicide Is *NOT* the Way to Happiness

Relieved, I thought back over some of the many times in my life that I had longed to leave this earth for a better place. I personally know how problems, large or small, can trigger feelings of depression and a desire to end it all. But there is no such thing as ending it all. If I didn't know what I know now and I still believed there was a nice, peaceful place to go to escape all worldly cares regardless of my actions, I'd probably be one of the first leading the parade to get there. But I *know* that is not the way to happiness on the Other Side.

My mind drifted along grim, macabre lines. What would this world be like and how empty would it be if all discouraged, depressed people killed themselves to escape to the Other Side?

Still, suicide, and my mistaken thoughts of the peace of death, had long been a part of my life. The thoughts had been planted like seeds in my mind when I was very young, growing quietly like a tumor, surfacing when times were difficult.

My thoughts turned to those earlier times and the myths I believed of the peace waiting for me in a beautiful place—regardless of my actions.

PART TWO

My Life

before Being

on the

Other Side

Chapter 3

∽

Rock Fights and Sleep Learning

In the Beginning

THINKING ABOUT MY CHILDHOOD brought painful memories. My mother married my father when she was a young girl hoping to find happiness by getting away from an unhappy home life. Shortly after they were married she became pregnant with me. It was during the depression in 1933, and another mouth to feed was a concern for my parents. Mother often told me how surprised and unprepared she was for my father's reaction when she told him of her pregnancy. He told her he only wanted the baby if it turned out to be a boy.

Well, I was a girl, and that did not help their chaotic relationship. Before I was a year old my father bundled our few clothes together and dropped us off at my grandparents' farm where Mother had grown up—the same farm she had tried so hard to get away from. My parents divorced shortly thereafter.

Childhood was not a pleasant time for me. It was difficult for my mother also, since she could not afford a baby-sitter and the only job she could get was cleaning a hotel. She desperately needed the work, so she took me to the hotel and left me by myself in a room down the hall from where she was working. I remember her telling me how hard it was for her when she received complaints from her employer about my crying.

From the time I was old enough to understand, I knew of our extreme financial difficulties and of the problems my mother had keeping and raising me. I hated myself for being born and becoming the cause of so much grief for my mother. I seldom saw my father while I was growing up and felt he had rejected me.

Over the years, hearing what a beautiful place the Other Side was made a vivid impression on me and added to my belief that dying and going there would be better than living. When I felt overwhelmed or depressed I would mistakenly think, "This life is temporary; there is a beautiful place where I can go when I die and I will be happy there." Death seemed a pleasant alternative to life and its problems.

Childhood Thoughts of Suicide

I don't remember how or when I first heard of a person taking their own life, but I distinctly remember thinking about suicide and what action I could take to kill myself when I was about eight years old. It started with foolish thoughts of wishing I had never been born and progressed to thinking I could *undo* life by ending it.

Soon, suicidal thoughts became habitual whenever I was confronted with unhappy circumstances. Such thoughts short-circuited my thinking and my ability to find solutions for problems. When difficult things happened, I could always fall back to the comforting notion that I did not have to stay in the situation and look for solutions. I bought into the myth of thinking that I could choose to die and go to eternal happiness whenever I wished.

In my younger years, I did not like school, and because my mother worked long hours, I was alone and unhappy most of the time when I *wasn't* in school. When my mother *was* home with me, I felt I was a burden that kept her from improving her lot in life. I felt great sadness as I saw schoolmates doing things with family and friends while I was at home feeling rejected, bored, and depressed. My unhappy thoughts compounded, and as I grew older, thoughts of suicide became more frequent.

Joyce at twelve years of age

An Army Helmet and Rock Fights

When I was twelve years old, I was very overweight, argumentative, and a real tomboy. Being overweight brought me a great deal of painful teasing, taunting (from bullies at school), and rejection. I was the brunt of almost everyone's humor. Having a lot of energy, I often used it in unproductive directions that brought me many hurtful experiences. It seemed I was always in a fight of some sort. Being a natural fighter both helped and hurt me. I even wore an army helmet that protected my head during rock fights with the neighbor kids. I didn't start them, but after they began, I hung in there until they ended.

Gradually, however, I lost a lot of my enthusiasm and kept to myself most of the time. When I was fifteen, I quit school for a short time, but soon discovered how much I did *not* know and found out that my lack of education hindered me in getting employment. Then I went back to school eager to learn.

Hiding from the World

By the time I was eighteen, my weight was normal and I had married, but not happily. My feelings of shyness intensified as I became more withdrawn than ever and shied away from people. My favorite outfit—a black scarf, a long maroon coat, and knee-high black galoshes with big zippers down the sides—made me feel invisible to the world.

Fear, dread of living, and feeling frightened of people were my constant companions, even when I wanted to go out to get the mail or the paper. I would peek out the drapes to see if anyone was around, then run out, get the paper or mail, and dash back into the house. My self-conscious and anxious feelings about meeting people or being seen by them were that intense—I was terrified of people!

On my nineteenth birthday I remember feeling exceptionally depressed. I felt "stuck," and I didn't see how my life could ever get any better. Because I loved youngsters, I began tending five children to earn money. Their mother was seriously ill, so I had them all the time, day and night. The children were extremely active, so tending them became an overwhelming task for an inexperienced nineteen-year-old with challenges of her own. The situation was demanding, but I did not realize things could get worse until all the children came down with chicken pox. I yearned for a better way of life.

A "New Me" Wanted

By the time I was twenty-four years old, I had stopped tending others' children; I had three of my own to care for—two girls and a boy. My marriage was falling apart, and I felt even more overwhelmed. Feeling that I had failed at life, I did not like myself at all. I was convinced that I was homely, unlikable, and that my situation could never improve. I wanted to change and have a new me, a new life. I prayed fervently and asked God to help me change—I felt as though I had to get away from me, but I didn't know how. My personal life continued to deteriorate, and I finally divorced. I felt almost numb to life.

Sleep Learning Transformation

God answered my prayers, however, and some big changes came into my life when I found a unique self-improvement course utilizing sleep-learning principles. The *learning-while-sleeping* courses promoted new ways of thinking and living; I developed new attitudes and confidence. I had not previously realized the importance of my thinking and how it influenced my behavior. I used the special recordings faithfully—bombarding my mind with positive, uplifting thoughts and suggestions for confident actions.

Before I Used Sleep Teaching Courses

After I Used Sleep Teaching Courses

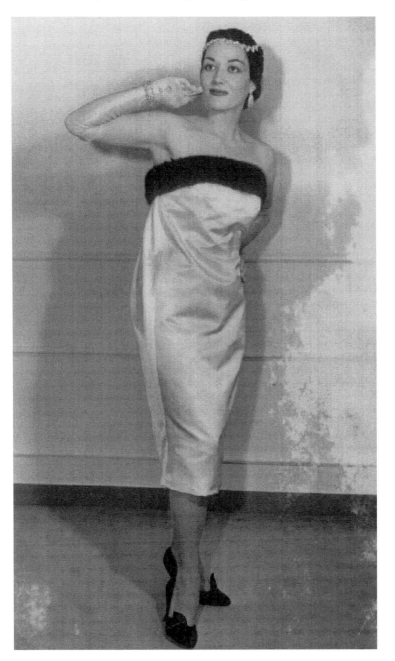

Sincere Interest in Others

I replaced negative thoughts of "I can't" with positive thoughts. I began looking for the good in people and situations around me rather than looking for and expecting the worst. With new thoughts in my mind of sincere interest in others, I overcame my fear of being around people.

As my thoughts, attitudes, and actions were significantly transformed, my whole life changed. After a few months of intense reconditioning of my thinking, I progressed from a fearful, insecure young woman to one studying additional self-improvement courses and doing professional modeling. In fact, the first time I modeled on television, I wore a swimsuit, and I wasn't even nervous. I truly had a new life and a new me.

"Being Thin"— a Current Fad

However, I had accepted society's current fad as truth: women had to be slender to be attractive. My weight went up and down, and whenever I gained weight and didn't fit the mold, I felt inferior and unhappy.

Being very weight conscious, I became thinner and thinner. In time, I was underweight and so slender that I wore a size five skirt held up by an elastic band. Even though I was 5' 5" tall and that thin, I still *felt* overweight.

Soon though, I realized that modeling did not offer a future for me. At that time, I had an attractive offer for a soft drink commercial, but it required going to a "private party" with the agent. There were other similar unacceptable requests so I withdrew from professional modeling.

Answered Prayers

Alone with three small children to raise, I was worried about meeting expenses. Then I received an unexpected phone call from my father. He helped me financially— enough that I could even purchase a house. I hadn't heard from him for quite some time, so his call and subsequent help and my new attitude, were all answers to prayers.

For a time, life seemed better. I had progressed a long way from rock fights in an army helmet and my long maroon coat. Yet, even though life was more enjoyable, nothing on earth seemed as attractive and appealing as the beautiful place I imagined the Other Side to be. I was eager to go there and still thought quite often about dying.

Chapter 4

⌖

My Trials Were Compounded

AT AGE TWENTY-SIX, I was injured in an auto accident with an aftermath of eight spinal surgeries drawn out from 1960 to 1975. I had four separate neck-fusion surgeries using five pieces of bone taken from my hips. I also had four low-back surgeries, including a massive bone fusion. Fortunately, I had insurance that covered most of the surgical expenses.

Around the time of my auto accident in 1960, however, my children began to develop health problems that ultimately required five surgeries. My son was only two when he developed a severe kidney infection—nephritis—that continued over the next few years. One day when I had him at the hospital for tests, I overheard the doctors discussing his case. They said that because of the recurring episodes of bleeding from his kidneys and the severity of his strep-throat infections which were related to the nephritis, he had only a fifteen-percent chance to live.

All three of my children had repeated and severe strep-throat infections. Several specialists told me it was critical for the children to have tonsillectomies, and that the girls had growths in their bladders that would also require surgery. At that same time my mother had surgery and was not able to help me, nor I her.

Many days I was in bed with my head and neck in traction and in so much pain that I could hardly move. My oldest daughter, Suzan, age seven, fixed us cereal or bread and milk for breakfast, lunch, and dinner. I felt as though I were drowning in problems and taking the children with me; I knew they needed better care.

It was very difficult for me, but since I was physically incapable of caring for my children, I decided to place them in the best foster homes I could find. Anguishing over my decision, I prayed they would understand that I was letting them go so their needs would be met. Foolishly, I blamed God for not giving me the health and home life for which I yearned.

An Unrecognized Blessing with Lasting Benefits

My youngest child, David, was about four years old when he left. To me, he was still my "baby boy" and I missed him terribly. Foster homes did not work out well for him until finally he went to live with an outstanding and highly respected family.

After he had been there about two years, I was still facing additional surgeries. David's foster family pressed me for permission to adopt him so they could give him the stability and home life he needed. I was extremely reluctant and made it a matter of fervent prayer. After some time, I had a definite answer that even though it was difficult for me, I was to let him go to them or David would not regain his health. So, with many tears, I agreed.

I could see that they sincerely loved him, and he was happy and well cared for there. I loved him too much to take him from them and bring him back into the chaos he would have with me. I missed him so, I thought my heart would break. However, with their loving care, his severe illness cleared up. He progressed and enjoyed life with a devoted father and mother who loved and provided for him as if he were their own.

Again, I thoughtlessly blamed God for the loss of my son, not recognizing that He had helped me with David. God saved David from the many heartaches he would have had if I had tried to keep him. (As an adult, David and I have a good relationship, and he has told me that he is grateful that I made the best decision for him.)

Inner Struggles

It was hard for the children to understand why they couldn't be with me and have the home life they wanted. They didn't understand why their mom was in the hospital or recuperating from surgery instead of being with them, and we all felt bad about it. My two daughters, Suzan and Patty, were in and out of foster homes and homes of relatives over the next several years as my health and personal problems continued.

Despite striving to maintain a positive attitude, my feelings of extreme discouragement increased. Years went by, and I wanted to escape my life's situations as I was trying to get the additional back surgery that I needed.

With the passing of time, my children grew to adulthood and married. We had good relationships with each other, but they lived in distant locales. They each had children, but circumstances and distance kept me from holding or enjoying my grandchildren. I ached inside but tried to appear cheerful to others and only cried when I was alone. I tried to help others around me find solutions to their problems rather than concentrating on what was wrong in my own life.

Hard Work with Winning Results

To earn income, I decided I would become a real estate agent when I saw the high demand for newly-built homes. I determined which company had the highest sales and made an appointment to apply. The sales manager who interviewed me was adamantly against women in sales with his company. For over three hours we had a "friendly debate" as he gave excuses why women would not do well selling houses not yet built, and I responded with reasons why women could do at least as well, or even better than men. Finally, he decided to let me try.

Two of the five other sales*men* in the office openly joked to each other about me working there, saying how foolish it was for me or any other woman to even attempt to compete with them. We all participated in a contest of the month with our names and the number of sales we made on a large blackboard in the office.

Concealing my painful back condition, I spent every free moment I could in the model home and calling on prospective leads. My hard work paid off when I won the contest for several months in a row. (Finally, the contest was terminated.) The two salesmen who had taunted me when I was hired, quit. I was surprised and pleased when I was introduced to the women who were their replacements.

My financial situation had improved considerably, but I was not able to keep up with the constant physical demands of selling real estate and was forced to resign. Not sure what direction my life would take, I continued my education by taking university classes when I could. Yet thinking about my future was still a big concern. More years of personal challenges went by as I kept studying and looking for ways to succeed in life.

My oldest daughter, Suzan, had three children. However, she had heartbreaking marital problems and finally ended her troubled marriage. She suffered a severe brain concussion and other injuries, and then attempted suicide and was no longer able to care for her children.

Her little girl, my granddaughter Crystal, was three years old and came to stay with me. My mother also came to live with me to help care for Crystal. Suzan's two other little ones, Ki, a boy eighteen months and Lorina, a baby girl, stayed with a loving couple since we were unable to care for them.

These were additionally difficult and challenging situations for all of us. But I had progressed to where I no longer blamed God for unwanted circumstances. I had begun to realize that most of my problems were linked to my choices or my family's choices and without God's blessings things could have been much worse.

Since I still had significant pain in my lower back, I consulted a specialist and surgeon who recommended and then performed spinal surgery. However, the results were painfully devastating with extensive complications.

It was over a year before I found an orthopedic surgeon who would agree to operate to try to correct what had been done to my back in the prior surgery. Afterwards, I was grateful that some relief was provided but more surgery was needed, and he would not agree to try again.

In 1975, I finally located a highly respected orthopedic surgeon who agreed to perform the needed lower-back surgery which required a bone fusion.

A week after the surgery, when I went home, I did not think my back pain could get any worse, but within about four weeks a more painful condition of undetermined cause set in. It progressed until I was taken back to the hospital by ambulance in excruciating and paralyzing pain from the small of my back down.

Additional specialists were called in, but to no avail. After weeks of the most sophisticated tests that were available at the time, it seemed that I would be permanently left in this agonizing state of existence with only the use of my arms, hands, mind, and voice. The muscles in my body were atrophying at an accelerating speed. My leg muscles hung shriveled and limp from my protruding bones.

The hospital's policy was that a patient could not remain in their care under hopeless conditions. My doctor, a renowned orthopedic surgeon, a marvelous man whom I greatly appreciated and respected, delivered this tragic message to me himself. I was told that my hospital room had to be vacated for someone with hope of recovery. A gurney was brought to take me by ambulance to a nursing home.

The staff and doctor seemed surprised at my reaction and response. I did not accept what I was told about my condition. Knowing how much Crystal and my mom needed me, I thoroughly believed I would recover and would even walk again.

Over the years with meditation and subconscious programming (Sleep Teaching) playing softly in the background even in the hospital, I had trained myself to believe in and receive miracles. I knew that somehow I would walk again. If I went to a nursing home at that time, I felt that I would become just a statistic, assigned a number waiting to die. I had other plans for my life. When my mental attitude was down and depressed, I wanted to die; when it was up, as it was then, I believed in miracles.

A quiet gloom seemed to fill the room; but undaunted, I asked the doctor if he believed in God. When he replied that he did, I said, "I need more time; I will walk again. I believe in miracles."

After a few seconds of silence, the staff, ambulance crew, and the doctor looked from one to another and left my room. As the door closed behind them, I closed my eyes and silently expressed my gratitude to God in prayer.

Chapter 5

~

Seeking Solutions and Making Progress

Having been granted additional time for recovery in the hospital, I didn't like just lying in bed being bored. I heard a nurse talking about a fun gift available on the east coast, a little plastic object being sold as a new type of "sea pet."

My mind was sparked with ideas. I thought of a pebble being a perfect, constant-companion pet. Most pets take a lot of care; this one would not. It was getting close to the holidays, and since I could not get out to shop, I thought this would make a good Christmas gift for some of my family and friends.

In spite of my pain, I felt exuberant as I thought of ideas about what to call these new pets and how to care for them. Not wanting to portray them as just plain old rock-pebbles, I wrote of them as unique pets. Suddenly I thought of their name, *Pedigreed Pet Pebbles.*™

They Bring Good Luck

Ideas continued coming to my mind. Grabbing a pen and paper, I began to write. The words flowed quickly: "Genuine, unique Pedigreed Pebbles™—the Perfect Pets."

I described how they could bring good luck, how loyal they were, and that they had a long life expectancy.

Then I began calling printers in the phone book until I found one who seemed to understand what I wanted. He laughed when he caught on to my idea and agreed to help me. He thought it would make a good gift for some of his family, too.

Eagerly, I called a cab to pick up my written pages to deliver to the printer. I did not realize the stir it would cause at the nurses station when the cab driver arrived and asked for directions to my room. I chuckled when the head nurse burst into my room unable to believe that I had called a cab when I couldn't even sit up.

I called a special friend, Shirley, and asked her to bring me some pebbles. When I got them I borrowed some scissors from the nurse and cut out little pieces of my lamb's wool mattress pad and glued them to the tops of the pebbles so they had "fur."

Finally, the day came when the little booklet was finished. It included copyrights, a story, and several cute illustrations. It seemed to catch people's interest and they encouraged me to make it available in stores.

Several buyers I called agreed to place my pets for sale in their stores. Over the phone, I ordered little bags to put the pebbles and manual in so they made a "ready to send" gift. Calling my friend Shirley again, I asked if she would bring me some things not usually brought to patients in the hospital: a few yards of fuzzy material, electric scissors, glue, and a huge container of pebbles; she laughed but agreed.

It was evening before she could get there with everything. Shirley helped stretch out the material in front of me and I cut it into strips. She put the pebbles all around me in the bed so I could reach them, and hung the strips on the metal trapeze-pull-bar over my head until I cut them into squares to glue onto the pebbles. Since it was nighttime, I thought we would have privacy and be left alone to work.

Lost in the Hospital Bed

Unexpectedly, the door opened and there stood a new specialist who had come to examine me. It was obvious he was not happy with what he saw. As he tried to turn me over to look at my back, he grumbled that there were books, rocks, and little pieces of material all around me. The doctor complained that this was the first time he ever had a problem *finding* a patient in a hospital bed.

My face burned with embarrassment but it did not diminish my enthusiasm for my new project. Shirley couldn't keep from snickering at these circumstances and the doctor's surprised reactions. When he left, she continued to help me and then gathered up the finished little pebbles which had dropped all around on the floor.

The next day, I made arrangements for someone to deliver them to the stores for sale. Those first *Pebble Pets* sold out quickly, and the stores wanted more—a few hundred-dozen more.

I was thrilled! *Pedigreed Pet Pebbles*™ it seemed, were a success. However, even when I offered to split the profits, I could not get ongoing help with this project. It was frustrating but I could not fill the orders. Shortly thereafter, *Pet Rocks,*™ a competitive product, came into the stores and I watched the sales figures climb out of sight.

Trying to console myself, I thought that maybe someday *Pedigreed Pet Pebbles*™ would be back. In the meantime, they would have to patiently wait to belong to their new owners.

My attention was once again focused on making it day by day and hour by hour. The pain in my back and down my legs was indescribable. However, I was determined to recover.

Logic vs. Faith

According to logic, reason, and medical science, I would never walk again; X-rays showed irreparable and permanent spinal damage. However, gradually and agonizingly, but miraculously, I forced, willed, and prayed movement and life into my back and legs. Bombarding my mind with positive suggestions—using Sleep Teaching continuously in the hospital—I welded the words into my mind and heart, "I will, I can walk again."

My thoughts focused on faith-promoting slogans such as, "As you believe, so shall you receive. Set your mind on a course and watch the world step out of your way for its accomplishment" (Napoleon Hill). And I grew stronger every day.

Slowly, I noticed a half an inch, then an inch of movement. With miracles, mental programming, and the use of a special medical device known as an *electrical-tens-unit* to decrease the pain, I eventually made enough progress to go home to a hospital bed in my living room. With the help of Mother and Crystal, who was four years old at the time, I continued my recovery at home. Though my condition was improved and there was hope, I was still quite helpless; if the house had caught on fire, I could not have gotten out of bed by myself.

Mother had a full-time job but managed to assist me. After breakfast, she put things within my reach that I needed for the day. She put Crystal's and my lunch in the refrigerator and made sure the phone was near. She brought me a large drink, enough to last for the day. Then she left for work until evening.

My Little Angel

I don't know what I would have done without my mother's and granddaughter's help. Crystal was loving and sweet like a little angel. Having her there lifted my spirits and helped me in many ways. She was so cheerful and cute with her dark hair and beautiful large blue eyes; it seemed she was always smiling. We played school and sang songs. Then she would watch TV.

Prayer and Mental Pictures

With the bed piled high with the phone, books, positive mind-programming materials, and things for me to keep working on, I tried to generate some income. All materials had to be within arm's reach for me to use. Crystal would get things for me that fell. I kept the Sleep Teaching recordings going continuously, programming my mind with the will and belief that I would accomplish my goals: I would walk again and succeed!

Later, doctors determined that after the last surgery, an undetected, disc-space infection had developed which was the source of my pain. I was given antibiotics, but I developed a reaction to them with side effects that caused permanent inner ear damage. This added other challenges of living in a world that shakes and spins all the time because I have lost my sense of balance, gravity, and direction. I had taken for granted these marvelous systems of the body—until they were gone.

The First Law of Learning Is Repetition

Studying, pondering, and meditating on scriptures and books filled with Great Universal Truths, I programmed them into my mind and heart. Fervently praying for miracles, I remember meditating and mentally picturing creative ideas and opportunities coming into my life. I knew that thoughts are creative, and I mentally pictured miraculous results. I knew the first law of learning is repetition, and I kept repeating what I believed would work.

A Business Idea

At that time, there had been many items in the news concerning severe energy shortages and a need for solutions to environmental health problems. This piqued my interest. I called schools, businesses, and governmental agencies for information explaining the problem and need for solutions.

One day the phone rang. It was an acquaintance telling me he knew of a successful businessman who was knowledgeable in these subjects. He told me my questions could probably be answered by this gentleman and arranged a luncheon appointment for us. I had been careful not to let the seriousness or the after-effects of my surgery be known. I knew that feelings of pity for my situation would not attract opportunities to me. He didn't even suspect I was still lying helplessly in a hospital bed in my living room. The businessman's time was flexible; I made our appointment for three weeks later.

Determination Creates Results

Thoughts of that waiting appointment helped me try harder every day until I could lift my head, sit up, and then with the help of a tight back brace, get up and walk. Finally, approximately two months after my release from the hospital, I kept that appointment and made it out of the house. Forcing back the tears, I cinched up my back brace extra tight, wore a long dress to cover my leg brace, and used a walking stick.

The businessman sent his chauffeur who helped me down the walk to the limousine and drove me to the meeting. They had no idea I could not have driven myself there at that time.

As we sat eating lunch and discussing revolutionary ideas, I braced myself against the arm of the chair trying to ease my pain. My back brace was cinched up so tightly to help hold me up that it almost cut off my breath, but I managed to conceal my discomfort.

At that meeting, I learned about potential opportunities for women-owned firms in the field of environmental health. Creative ideas came into my mind that seemed workable. This opportunity seemed a tangible answer to my prayers. The businessman wished me luck on my new quest for further information and had his chauffeur drive me back home.

Belief Leads to Action

Believing in the potential of my new venture, I obtained another loan on the house and the money enabled me to begin searching for a way to accomplish my goals. Also, I received training as a professional consultant.

With new crutches, back braces, leg braces, and the medical tens-unit that sent electrical stimulation to my spine to help ease the pain, my travel and search for environmental solutions in the high-technology industry began. I believed that *ingenuity* + *courage* + *work* = *luck and opportunity, and that luck* + *opportunity* + *faith* = *miracles*. With determination, I started on a new adventure.

In 1980 my mother retired from her employment and purchased a mobile home. She and Crystal (who was then nine years old) moved. I missed them but it improved our relationship. When we lived in the same house, it seemed my mom and I were constantly having disagreements.

While working to obtain the sought-after contracts, I received many negative comments such as, "Why don't you go back to the kitchen and leave complicated things to men." And "Women were never meant to work in a man's world." And, "What makes you think you can do this? Women can't work in a man's field." Those comments hurt but did not deter me.

Keep On Keeping On

Forging ahead was not easy, but I felt I had to "keep on keeping on." During this period of time, however, I not only walked on my own, but traveled to many areas and met with many interesting and knowledgeable people. Pursuing my education, including specialized training, I learned about environmental health solutions for private industry and governmental agencies.

My efforts paid off, and I obtained a valuable twenty-year government contract. The future seemed secure for me and my family, and I was enthusiastic about it as I received recognition from experts in the fields of high-technology and environmental health.

Contracts and Cash Flow

The project proceeded successfully from 1978 through 1980 and held even more promise as other communities requested similar contract information. A division of a large corporation I had hired as my agents and the project administrators took care of the accounting and a significant cash flow, and I relied on them. Together, we addressed the concerns of the employees, politicians, and the community. I worked hard coordinating engineering, organizing the projected construction, and arranging the financing.

My agents took charge of the money and at the time, I believed in their figures. My contract with them provided that I receive a percent of the net; I did not realize that the net amount could be "adjusted." There were always complicated excuses for why there was never much left over. I was under tremendous stress to keep the project running smoothly and "next year" was always promised for the project's "real" funds to be coming in that would benefit me and let my company develop as projected.

I was encouraged to "go develop other projects" since this one was coming along so successfully. Believing my agents were taking care of things at the project, I worked at becoming more knowledgeable in health concerns and in technology for the project's expansion.

Gaining Knowledge and Confidence

I had regained my health to a remarkable degree. Now, no one could tell by my outward appearance that I still had a lot of back pain and problems with my balance. I had worked at concealing these conditions to the point that it was extremely difficult for me to admit that I had pain or needed medical care.

Knowing this, my physician gave me a letter to carry when I traveled explaining that I understate my problems with pain. Also, because of having severe labyrinthine dysfunction (balance problems) he gave me a letter which explained that I was not precluded from driving, even though walking was difficult for me. (I still carry up-dated letters in case of an emergency.)

When I was able, I attended international business conferences and gained valuable knowledge as I studied advanced technology and went to specialized seminars. It was fascinating listening to and interacting with top scientists from all over the world as they discussed solutions to environmental health and hazard problems.

Opportunities were abundant to provide needed solutions working with some of the leading engineers in the world such as Ellis Armstrong, past Commissioner of the Bureau of Reclamation and past Chairman of the World Energy Conference, who had additional widely recognized achievements. With a team of other such knowledgeable and professional experts from companies such as Dow Chemical Co. and E.F. Hutton, I was eager to develop other potential projects.

Joyce, as a businesswoman, in the summer of 1981

PART THREE

My Experience
in the
Spirit World

Chapter 6

∼

Challenges and a "Ticket to Paradise"

FROM MY TRAUMATIC HEALTH problems and from my work experiences, I had learned the value of hope and working for a worthwhile cause. My faith and my desire to succeed in the promising work opportunities kept me going. Being actively involved and continuing my education kept me from dwelling on my many physical problems and helped my mental well being. As my knowledge increased, so did my confidence.

Then in December 1981, I awakened late one night with a severe pain in my right eye. A dim nightlight cast the only glow in my dark bedroom. As I was getting up to find out what was wrong with my eye, I found that my leg muscles wouldn't support me. In the near-darkness, I lost my balance and fell. My face struck something on the floor that fractured my skull in two places around my left eye socket. However, my attention was predominately on the pain in my right eye. It felt as though a large foreign object of some kind were in it.

The next morning, I went to an ophthalmologist. After examining my eye, the doctor put a patch over it saying I had scratched the cornea. He said he would not know for ten days whether I would lose the vision in it. X-rays showed the skull fractures. Nothing could be done for the swelling and fractures around the left eye.

Hardly believing this was happening to me, I nervously laughed when I looked in the mirror at myself with a swollen, black eye on the left and a big patch on the right. It became even more of a struggle to be positive and to avoid feeling sorry for myself.

Joyce in December of 1981

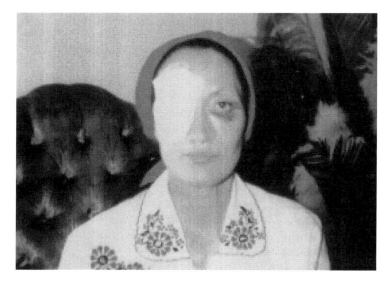

Later, I learned these were some of my better days for a long time to come!

I was assured by my agents that my presence was not needed at the project. A bleak and lonely Christmas came and went while I was not only house-bound with pain, but worried that I might be losing my vision. On New Year's Eve, I was still confined to the house, not at all happy with what was going on. That evening, I was sitting in my living room pondering my situation, feeling sad that I had missed all the possible fun of the holidays.

Feeling water dripping on me, I looked up and saw the ceiling over my head sagging. With a shock I realized that the roof was leaking. I had replaced the roof only three years before—an expensive, messy job I didn't want to go through all over again.

Pushed to the Edge

Everything seemed to be pushing in on me at once: my loneliness, the stress associated with my business and lack of money, the severe pain in my back, the possible loss of my vision, and now the leaking roof. I sat in the chair pondering the many problems that weighed on me while I watched the water falling on the furniture. My habit of thinking I wanted to escape my earthly challenges resurfaced as I thought, "Oh, let me out of here; I want to die. I just want to die."

While I was still recovering in January, 1982, I fell again. I went down hard and broke my tail bone. It hurt terribly. (Later, my muscle weakness that caused my falls was diagnosed as Myasthenia Gravis—Muscular Dystrophy—and more.)

Respiratory infections began plaguing me, and I was frequently bedridden with one illness after another. I would get a sore throat and be unable to get over it. The doctors weren't sure what to do as I began having severe reactions to the prescribed antibiotics. I began hurting and aching all over. My muscles were weak and I had trouble swallowing. If I cannot get well, I thought again, I just want to die.

Wanting Peace in a Beautiful Place

Believing in God and Heaven, I wanted to go to that beautiful place and have the peace of mind I had heard others tell about. *I began praying that I would die.* As time passed, I became physically worse with episodes of intense sweating followed by intense chilling. Also, I developed an allergic reaction to the chemicals in my clothing. In fact, many items in my environment that had never bothered me before would trigger a series of sweatings that would leave me drenched, and then I would chill.

Many days Mother came to take care of me. To battle the sweating and chilling, I changed my clothes several times a day. It took much of my strength, along with her help, for me to have dry clothes—and to just exist. Some special friends and neighbors often shopped for me and brought in meals.

Striving to overcome these ailments, I wanted to believe that any day things would get better. I wanted to conceal my illness. I had been assured by my agents that they were competently working in my behalf and that I was being properly represented at all meetings; I was told that my presence was not necessary. Not feeling needed by anyone, I avoided contact with friends and associates except for phone calls when I was feeling well enough to talk.

My condition fluctuated, but I became progressively worse. The doctors couldn't tell me what was wrong without running extensive tests. Since I no longer had insurance, I could not afford the tests.

Give Me This Day . . . *Lasting Peace in Death*

As the pain became more severe, I began asking caring friends to pray with me that I could die and be released from these trials. They told me they were praying for God's will to be done. They also said that as they prayed they felt that I was going through these trials for a purpose, but that I would have my choice to live or die. I had made my choice. I wanted to die!

The bronchitis and respiratory infections continued. Then I began bleeding from up inside my head and down my throat. I would wake up in the mornings almost unable to breathe. Consulting an ear, nose, and throat specialist, X-rays showed no medical problems, and the doctor could not pinpoint any cause for my problems.

A whole year had gone by since I started this downward spiral. It was December 1982 and I was still painfully alive. Believing that my family didn't really need me anymore, I continued to wish I could die naturally and be released from this living hell called life. The pain in my joints and body increased, and I could walk only by bracing myself on furniture.

Ticket to Paradise

In January 1983, a doctor I greatly respected performed some tests that revealed I had a low white-blood count so I was not fighting off the infections; I would continue to get worse. Also, I was informed that the tests revealed I had rheumatoid arthritis; in a short period of time I would be in a wheelchair, never to walk again. By having increasing pain and being bedridden with worsening rheumatoid arthritis and a low white-blood count not fighting the continued infections, I would most likely get pneumonia and die a natural death.

On the day I heard this news, I believed God was handing me my ticket to paradise. I wouldn't have to commit suicide—I thought I would just die. I was happier than others would be if they had unexpectedly won tickets to Hawaii.

It was physically difficult that day to take my shower; but feeling so elated about dying gave me a little extra energy. I was fantastically happy that I was going to die and go to my imagined place of "forever happiness and joy." As the water sprayed over me, I was thinking of how wonderful I was going to feel when I left all my problems behind.

A song joyfully came to my mind and I sang parts of it: *Somewhere over the rainbow . . . where troubles melt like lemon drops, away above the chimney tops, that's where you'll find me.* The words and melody of that tune stayed in my mind for hours and lulled me to sleep that night with pleasant thoughts of my coming "trip." Those words portrayed the new attitude I had for the next few days.

My dying, I thought, would take a little time and that was okay! It meant I would be able to complete my earthly affairs, such as making my burial arrangements. I would have to do them slowly because I was so ill. Still, I wouldn't leave my family in chaos, and that was important to me. I believed it would be much better for my loved ones when I died.

Snapshot taken by Crystal, my granddaughter, a few days before
I went to the Other Side—January, 1983

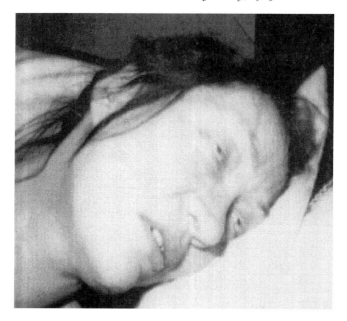

Chapter 7

~

I Went to the Spirit World

A FEW DAYS LATER, I felt weaker and more ill than ever. I was alone that day. As the morning wore on, I continued to feel much worse. I began worrying and thought, I can't die yet; I'm not quite ready.

I wanted to pray, but was too weak to kneel on my own. The bathroom was large and attractive with an ivory-marbled tub and white-lace shower curtains. I decided I would use the edge of the bathtub to lean on. I managed to get into the bathroom even though the pain in my body was intense, and I had lost most of my strength. Supporting myself by leaning over the side of the tub, I maintained as reverent a posture as I could to pray.

I Wanted to Die—But Not Yet

I wanted to pray for just enough strength to finish a few critical tasks before I died. I bowed my head in prayer but before I was able to formally ask, I heard a voice as distinct and clear as if the speaker were standing directly above me. The voice said, powerfully, "If you come, you come now!"

With that, my strength left me and I slumped forward. All the air went out of me as I felt a sinking heaviness in my body. With a swoosh up and outward, I left my body and found myself behind and slightly elevated from my body, my feet not touching the floor. I felt weightless and the physical pain was gone.

Spiritual Shock

I had thought that when people die, they went through a tunnel away from the world with its challenges and its problems to the beautiful, happy place I'd heard about— but I did not. I was shocked that death and dying was not what I had expected it to be. The room seemed to have no limitations to my view as I looked up, around, and then down. Looking down, my attention focused on my body slumped lifelessly over the tub.

Immediately, I noticed the difference between seeing myself from the mirror's flat surface to observing my body's shape as another person could see it including a total view from the back. Looking around, I realized that my sight was not limited to the use of my eyes. I could see 360 degrees around me. I had always thought of vision as occurring in the one direction I focused on. But I could see behind me and in front as well as above me. In this sphere, there was sort of an instant visual awareness of everything around me.

I felt wispy, almost transparent. I was aware that I could go through a wall and my hand could go through anything. I was also very aware of my limitations without my body; the knowledge was simply there. Anything I had not said while on earth would remain unsaid, anything I had not written while on the earth would not be written. I could not pick up anything—not even a piece of paper.

Heavenly Hologram

It is difficult to describe what happened next. Events did not slowly progress from one phase to another as they had when I was alive on earth. Everything seemed to be happening almost instantaneously. Consequently, it is difficult to separate this experience into periods of time or to differentiate it into stages. The Other Side's dimension and my experiences there were as a whole, like a hologram. God's universe was complete; it was magnificent beyond belief and absolutely beyond earthly description.

Vast knowledge and immeasurably deep feelings relating to my own personal development accompanied everything I experienced on the Other Side. This was the most vivid, personal experience I have ever known. I have struggled to find the right words to share this marvelous, yet extremely anguishing experience.

The Spirit World Is Real

Vividly aware I was in a spiritual realm, I knew I was in a sphere of afterlife, a place without my body, a space and time before resurrection. I had not realized there were distinct phases of afterlife—the spirit world when I would be *without* my body, and resurrection when my spirit and body would be reunited.

This different realm was more realistic, authentic, and factual to me than earth-life's sphere. This was, without question, the most stark, real thing I had ever experienced. All else seemed insignificant in comparison; but I was shocked that nothing in the spirit world was as I expected it to be.

Everything fit with a sharp reality, however, and with new knowledge in my mind. I had read in the Bible that the spirits of some people who had died long before Christ's resurrection were finally reunited with their bodies after *His* resurrection. I realized that they must have been in a wispy, spirit world similar to this one until the time of their resurrection.

A desperate longing for my physical body overwhelmed me as I realized how terribly limited I was without it. I wanted to communicate with my family, to tell them I loved them and missed them, but I could not.

My chance on earth was over, and now it was too late. I realized with feelings of remorse that what I had thought of as dying and being in a state of "paradise" was not at all as I had anticipated.

Chapter 8

≈

In the Presence
of God's Light and Love

SUDDENLY, I WAS IN the presence of a beautiful Personage who radiated an overpoweringly brilliant white light. I knew that my natural eyes could not have endured this light. His Presence was brighter than anything I could have imagined. He was glorious and inspiring—radiant with love. I was filled with an awesome knowledge about God, His power, and His love. It permeated my whole being, and I received my own special witness that Jesus IS the Christ, the Son of God, and He is filled with saving grace.

How humbling! I felt I should bow or kneel to show my reverence. I had always loved my Creator, but I had never felt an actual personal relationship with Him.

While in the Presence of this Personage of Light, I was instantly and keenly aware of the fact that **God is real!** I was also keenly aware of a definite purpose for life. New understandings and meanings of life's happenings flooded my mind. And I knew that earth life is the time to repent and prepare to meet God. *I was given heavenly answers for earthly challenges.*

God's Love

My love for God was greater than I had thought possible, beyond my earth-life's comprehension. I realized God loved me unconditionally and that He knew all about me. My own self-awareness of my thoughts and actions was sharply intensified. I wanted to shrink away from God and His Presence of love and truth. I felt great anguish, remorse, and sorrow for things I had done in life that I knew I should not have done, and for things I knew I ought to have done that I did not do while I was alive on earth.

As my understanding increased, my love for the Creator of the universe increased. I felt an overwhelming appreciation for the blessings I had received in earth life. However, the more that I realized the opportunities I had in life, the more my anguish intensified for having not used my time on earth better.

The Personage standing before me radiated such a bright light it was difficult to make out particular features. But He was powerful, all knowing, and so loving. I felt His unconditional love radiating throughout my mind and soul. I had no idea there could be so much love for or from anyone, or that I had the ability to have these deep feelings of love for someone else. Instantly I knew that people do not have to be in a high-ranking position in earth life for God to love them. His love is boundless, limitless. He loves everyone, and I realized how important all of us are to Him.

I thought of loving someone with an intense and all encompassing emotion, the most love anyone could ever feel for a child or a companion, and I knew *that* love is nothing compared to the love we have for our Creator as we come to know Him.

The Ultimate Joy—
Being in His Presence

My earlier thinking was that if I could have a moment with God, or someone representing Him, there would be many questions I would like to ask. But I discovered I didn't desire to ask Him anything. I just wanted to enjoy His presence, to bask in His love, to be with Him.

Then I thought about being reunited with loved ones after a long separation. All I would want is to be in their presence, to love them, to feel their love for me in return. Bringing them up to date on events or quizzing them would seem foolish.

Feeling encircled in this love was a wondrous experience. I knew that the most horrible thing that could ever happen to me, my family, friends, or any of us who knew God would be to do something that would cut us off from His Presence. To be anywhere else but in that presence would truly be hell.

With new-found understanding of God's love, I knew I had let Him down. As I realized this, my understanding was opened. Knowledge flooded my consciousness and thousands of different subjects instantaneously lit up my comprehension. This experience simply defies explanation.

Inner Awakening

It wasn't that this knowledge was coming from an outward source—it was as though knowledge which had always been within me was awakened. It was as if, in an instant, a cloud evaporated from my mind and I had access to more knowledge and understanding than I had ever imagined. I knew my Creator was all knowing, all powerful, and able to reveal all needed things to my view.

In Scriptures and Holy Writings many great truths are taught in symbolic parables; perhaps some of the things I was shown were visual parables of great truths. I saw things I was familiar with used as representations of concepts. I saw these concepts as complete blocks, not merely as words. Words were not necessary and thoughts were simply known and didn't need to be spoken.

Pure and higher forms of communication took place

there—mostly through thoughts. By comparison, earth-life communications seemed limiting and archaic. The free flow of ideas and instant understanding were so much quicker and clearer in the spirit realm. It was communication from mind to mind, being to being.

God-Given Answers

Always-present knowledge, Eternal Truth that in some way constantly surrounds us, was revealed to me. I understood that many of these Eternal Truths are also available during earth life, although they are not easily perceived. They are available when the time is right and an individual is willing to make a deliberate effort to tune into the right wavelength. I was filled with a stark reality of knowledge. I discovered there is no new truth. Truth is eternal and ever-present.

Suddenly, the answers to questions and challenges I had in life came so quickly and seemed so obvious, I felt repentant for even wondering. I understood *reasons* for problems and *answers* to problems. I immediately yearned to come back to earth life and share what I had learned with my family, loved ones, and others.

Sands in an Hour Glass

Also, I was aware I had *created* an anguishing hell for myself, because I could have done more with my time on earth than I did. I knew that *time*, as it was known on earth, was limited, running out like sands in an hour glass beginning at birth and continuing until death. Time was to be used wisely and however it was spent, it could not be called back. Earth life was the foreign sphere, and time on earth was temporary, limited, and precious!

Thinking of some of the people I had known in my life who had wasted a lot of their time hurting others, I realized that God sorrowed when they did wrong, but He still loved them. Feeling great sadness for them, I realized how they were really hurting themselves. I understood that each person has a definite purpose for living and only so much earth time to fulfill that purpose.

Challenges and Rewards

Viewing my own life's experiences, I saw that learning self-control is a great challenge and takes time. Some of the greatest strengths we can develop are those required to control feelings and emotions, *especially the strength required to harness the tongue.* However, I saw rich, eternal rewards such as better family relationships that could be reaped by striving to master these things.

I knew that every act of kindness carries a reward. It was amazing to me that *even little kind acts could reap very large rewards.* Every good attitude, everything right I had ever done in my physical body had been a gift to God and to me.

My new understanding included knowing that any wrong deed I had done with unrighteous motivation or intention was actually hurting *me.* Many rewards that could have been mine were lost because of my own actions or my sins of omission. I was shown how everything I did during my earth life had consequences; every action I took had a definite reaction and brought an appropriate reward or a just punishment—a cause and effect, as if I were planting seeds and reaping exactly what I sowed.

Planting and Reaping

Scenes flashed quickly before my view and I saw farmers of all eras—weary, medieval peasants tilling the ground with crude stick-tools, others dragging wooden plows; then futuristic, sophisticated machines crawling over immense fields, row after row, field after field, planting seeds. My interest and attention was not on the farmers or their surroundings; I was fascinated with the seeds and the miracles of growth connected to them.

Time was compressed. No sooner had they planted than they began harvesting what they had sown. Those who planted corn reaped corn, those who planted carrots reaped carrots. Those who planted rice reaped rice. Someone planting carrots would not reap apples. Whatever was planted was harvested—in its own kind.

This Life Is the Time to Plant

Rapidly, these scenes appeared to my view. Then the scenes changed, and now people were harvesting love and kindness because they had sown love and kindness with their intended actions, while beside them others were reaping hateful, hurt feelings and violence, because they had sown hate and hurting of others with their intent and actions.

Every kindness, every right decision, every forbearance was returned in kind; every cruel act, every hurtful decision, every quick-tempered retort reaped a like result. All the time these scenes were playing before my view, I recalled a proverb I had heard during earth life: *As ye sow, so shall ye reap.* (Galatians 6:7)

The messages of the scenes I viewed became clear to me: forgiveness reaps forgiveness, mercy reaps mercy, love reaps love, violence reaps violence—the harvest of anger at others is anger directed at oneself. The eternal truth is that no one can escape harvesting what they plant.

Then I knew that earth life is a time to plant, and the Other Side is the ultimate time of the law of the harvest—as we give, so shall we reap. I was reaping anguish because of what I had sown during my earth life. I had made my own choices in life as to how to think and act. With my thoughts, actions, and *reactions* to situations and to others' actions I had created for myself what I was receiving. I had not realized that while I was alive on earth I had been building my character, my spiritual being, and determining my own harvest of eternal rewards, or lack thereof. I discovered that I *chose* joy or agony by my thoughts and actions during my earth life.

Also, I had a vivid awareness that studying Scriptures and Holy Writings would have revealed great truths that were grand keys to solving problems, achieving lasting peace of mind and eternal enjoyment.

During my earth life, my love and knowledge of the Great Creator of the Universe was limited, but now I was filled with His love for me and mine for Him. My love and gratitude to Him for my many blessings seemed endless; my love for others was increased—it was all-encompassing—and I realized how important we all are to each other. Again, I was filled with anguish for not having used my time on earth more productively. I had wasted precious time wanting to die.

Being in the presence of this Personage of Love and Light made me wish I had used every minute I had on earth planting love so I could reap blessings.

Chapter 9

~

A Spirit Contorted in Sorrow and Pain

SUDDENLY, I SEEMED TO be transported through time with scenes quickly passing my view. Then I was in a chapel with flowers everywhere—large beautiful bouquets on pedestals. The room was crowded with somber people; the only sounds were soft whispers and muffled sobbing. I could see everyone there, but they could not see me and no one reacted to my presence.

Glancing around, I saw a line of mourners filing slowly past a modest casket. The body of a young woman with shoulder-length, strawberry-blond hair lay in the casket. Mortuary skills and cosmetics had given her a placid expression; she looked peaceful and beautiful. How sad, I thought—such a young woman robbed of everything earth life had to offer.

My view then focused on an older woman sitting off to one side. She seemed dazed, her eyes staring into space. The pain emanating from her was undeniable. I knew at once she was the dead woman's mother, hurting as any parent would when burying one's child. Two beautiful little girls, perhaps four and six years of age, were with her. They were daughters of the deceased woman and this woman's grandchildren, and they were sobbing uncontrollably. Their hair had been lovingly done by a caring relative and they were both dressed in frilly, blue dresses with white lace trim.

Somehow, I knew these dresses had been purchased by their dear mother for a happy occasion in the recent past. Now they were being worn for her funeral. The youngest child sat on her grandmother's lap, clinging to her and weeping desperately. The six-year-old stood at the side of the grandmother, her face buried in her hands. Her little shoulders shook with her sobs. The children could not stop crying, but their grandmother, in such pain she hardly seemed to realize they were there, was unable to offer comfort.

I understood her thoughts: How was she ever going to take the place of the children's dead mother? She was older, with few financial resources and even fewer physical resources on which to draw. How could she ever love them enough to ease the pain of losing a mother who had left them by choice?

The Anguish of Reaching Out in Vain

The dead woman had not died in a tragic accident or of disease. This knowledge came vividly to my mind. She had taken her own life, died by her own actions, voluntarily giving up her chance to accomplish anything more during earth life.

Suddenly, I saw the spirit of the young woman kneeling at her mother's feet. She was different from the others in the chapel. Her body was not full and solid as were the bodies of her mother and children and the other mourners. She was wispy and transparent as I was at that moment—a spiritual body, not a physical one—and her face was contorted in sorrow and pain. Her mortal body lay a few feet away in the coffin, yet her essence, her spirit, her soul was here, sobbing at her mother's knees. I heard her thoughts, her words. She was sorry, oh, so sorry, for what she had done to them. She ached for them and the pain they were experiencing because of her actions.

She reached out, unable to touch them or to be felt by them. Her desperate attempts to make herself heard or understood failed utterly. She tried to take the oldest girl into her arms to comfort her; she wanted to console, to caress her children, but they didn't even know she was there.

I listened as she begged their forgiveness. She was desperate to make them understand, but they could not hear her words. All she could do was watch in torment as they suffered from her actions. I realized she had been a single mother raising these little girls alone. The emotional and physical responsibilities had overwhelmed her; she had come to the point where she felt that her problems and pressures were too great to endure. She felt depressed and allowed her feelings of despondency to grow to the point that she mistakenly felt that release from life was her only solution.

The Tragedy of Death By Choice

She had committed suicide thinking she would find peace—and sometime in the future she probably will find forgiveness and peace. But for now, she instead found misery as she helplessly watched the pain she had inflicted on the ones she so loved. Instead of being free from emotional strife, she was feeling intensified sorrow, compounded with regret for what she had done to her family. I could sense her agonized frustration—she was unable to communicate with or console her loved ones. She was utterly helpless to aid them in any way.

(In suicide, as in all things, only God is the ultimate judge and will decide the degree to which each person is accountable for their actions.)

A View of the Future

As I watched the scene, my view changed and I envisioned the girls begin to grow up, raised by their grandmother. Their dead mother continued observing their progress and their pain as they grew up without her. Her torment was great as she saw how they needed her, longed for her, hated her, and dealt with the fact of their mother's abandonment (which they perceived as rejection) at every stage of their lives.

She saw her children's sorrow and how she had personally handicapped them. And when they would need her, she would be unable to reach them with her love. Physically she would not be there for them—never could be there for them. How she longed to hold them. She wished she could undo her death and return to her children. I understood that she would watch, not only her children, but others in her life who had been wounded by her choice to kill herself.

The Ripple Effect

The analogy of a pebble thrown into a pond came to mind. The ripple that results expands outward and ultimately affects an area immeasurably larger than the size of the pebble itself; the ripple travels on and on. I understood that every action in life, especially suicide, affects so many people that its effect seems endless. The ripples—often more like tidal waves—caused by the deed roll outward, touching many lives.

My Personal Hell

Having willed myself to die, akin to suicide in my case, I knew that my inner hell would be viewing the loved ones I had left, witnessing the repercussions of my actions. Such thoughts stayed with me throughout my experience. It would be my own personal hell seeing and not being able to alleviate the sorrow that my actions caused. I was my own judge and was now judging from the Spirit World's all-seeing, all-knowing perspective.

The knowledge that I could have done better was agonizing. Seeing my attitudes and actions in the light of truth was misery to my soul. I yearned to warn my family and others of the regret and anguish that I was experiencing. Intensely I wanted to return to my mortal life and again have the privilege of living in my physical body even with its pain and illnesses—even with the same conditions I had sought to escape for so many years.

The Tragedy of Teen-Age Suicide

As quickly as I grasped this, I was shown another scene. Again, I was at a funeral, viewing a person who was deceased. I was standing at the head and slightly behind a beautiful, very expensive casket made of rich rosewood. I knew that this entire funeral had been elaborately expensive and that the high cost of the funeral was an attempt of grieving parents to soothe their pain.

As I watched, again no one seemed aware of my presence. Before me stood four mortal beings and a spirit personage. I understood at once who each person was and what they were feeling. Standing next to me was the spirit personage of a young man. His form, like that of the young mother I had previously seen, was wispy, nearly transparent. He was a good-looking teenager with sandy-colored hair cut short. His natural intelligence was apparent.

Wanting to Make Contact

An exact duplicate of his form lay in the open casket directly in front of me. I looked from one to the other in amazement. In contrast to his spirit self, his mortal body was solid, still, and lifeless. Its facial features were peaceful, as if he merely slept. His spirit face was contorted with torment and despair. Desperately wanting to make contact, he was reaching out his insubstantial, wispy arms to his father who was gazing down at the body in the casket. His father's shoulders were stooped from almost unbearable sorrow, his face drawn, his eyes swollen from crying.

Somehow I knew many things about this man. He was close to retirement with limited financial resources. He had stretched himself beyond his means to make this funeral elaborate, using money from his retirement funds for this final farewell, sparing no expense in an attempt to ease his grief.

The boy's mother stood at the foot of the casket weeping quietly. Her pain and confusion were profound. The father was speaking softly to two young men; I sensed that they were best friends of the dead boy. Handsome young men, they were intelligent, personable, and well dressed. I realized they were leaders in their classes at school and that they seemed perplexed.

Thoughts about Futility Are Futile

What impressed me as I focused on these two young men was the depth of depression and hopelessness they both had been feeling for some time. The death of the youth did not create, but simply brought to the surface, their feelings of futility—the same feelings the deceased boy had felt when he took his life. I had wasted a large portion of my life feeling the same way.

The father was telling the friends that his dead son had been a troubled boy with many problems. He looked down at his son's body and rested his hand on the edge of the casket as he said, "He's at peace now." This was what the mourning friends and family wanted to hear. These words eased their sorrow and made this loss easier to bear.

"No, Dad!" the boy's spirit cried out, "Stop! Don't tell them that." I watched as his spirit tried desperately to gain his father's attention, and with horror I realized why he was trying so hard to communicate with his dad.

False Hope

The bereaved father continued talking about his son having gone to a better and happier place. He told them his son was free from the pain and depression he felt while alive. I realized the father's words that he wanted to believe were true gave feelings and thoughts of false hope to the two young friends that they could find peace if they, too, committed suicide.

For these boys, the father's words were an invitation to join their friend—a confirmation of what they wanted to be true. They wished to believe that their friend was finally at peace, was finally free from his problems and sadness. They hoped that they, too could find that peace. The father's words of self-comfort reinforced that message.

But their dead friend was trying with all his might to communicate to them that he was *not* at peace. He could see the way his friends were feeling—the father could not. Each boy was struggling within, making the decision whether to continue in a life he felt was hopeless or to kill himself and find this beckoning peace. The spirit boy faced his friends in frustration, knowing they couldn't hear him. I heard him wail, his fists clenched, as he tried to communicate with them and convince them not to believe what his father was saying. "My father is wrong, so wrong," he kept saying.

The Lie of "Peace through Suicide"

The father continued speaking about how his son had wanted peace and freedom from worldly cares and that now he had it. The son's spirit-facial features became even more contorted as he shrieked, "No peace, I have no peace!" He was futilely trying to communicate with his father, and trying to warn his friends not to make the same mistake. If they did, he knew his misery would be even worse.

Feelings of misery seemed to exude from him. He had taken his own life, falsely believing that in death he would find happiness, peace, and contentment. He thought he could escape from all earthly anxiety—instead he found feelings of intense sorrow and anguish that were greater than any he had experienced when he was alive.

He began sobbing, and I observed that the son found absolutely no comfort in the beautiful funeral. Instead he felt great misery in the "reassuring" words his father spoke. He understood clearly that it wasn't only these two close friends that would be impacted by his actions and his father's words.

Suicide Is NOT the Answer!

If one or both of these boys chose to die, there would be family, other friends, peers, and schoolmates affected. Even strangers who would hear about his death or read the obituaries might be influenced into thinking suicide was a solution. I saw how feelings of hopelessness could compound, affecting many people, sweeping onward relentlessly like waves driven by storms far across the ocean.

I felt great sorrow for the dead boy who had given up his chance at earth life, great sorrow for the friends who were seriously contemplating taking their own lives, and for the parents who had invested so much time and love in their son. A feeling of anguish swept over me and I wanted to run away as I recognized how my own life fit a pattern similar to what I had been shown. I felt overwhelmed with feelings of guilt, and *I knew suicide was not the answer!*

Suicide—a Disease?

Thinking suicidal thoughts, as I had so many times, often leads to the act of committing suicide. *Suicide is like a disease* that kills some and often cripples everyone else involved. Suicide and the hopeless feelings of depression connected to it, snowball from sad individual to sad individual. Suicide begins cycles of negative thoughts and feelings that create misery throughout generations, robbing posterity and all concerned of great might-have-beens of joy, accomplishments, and peace of mind.

Chapter 10

~

A Lightning-Speed Life Review

As I WAS BEING shown things in the Spirit World, suddenly, with lightning speed, my whole life began unfolding before me. I felt again the emotions I experienced during the actual times I first lived them. I was aware of the overall circumstances, aware that I was now in a different time and spiritual domain than on earth when they first took place. The people I saw in my life review were not wispy, as were the spirits I'd seen. They looked rounder, more solid and natural, as mortal beings.

Instead of the limited perspective I'd had on earth, this experience encompassed the feelings and viewpoints of all those involved, including the Creator's. With this perspective came a stark, resounding realization: life had not been the way it was portrayed in movies, books, songs, or newspapers. Life had not been as I had perceived it at all!

A Reality Check

In the Spiritual Sphere, I had a new, sharp awareness of reality. My life review continued, bringing with it an awareness of the feelings and perspectives of those with whom I had associated throughout my life. I was aware of the way they felt about my actions and our interactions. The review was difficult but informative. I experienced many and varied emotions. I was amused to realize that many situations I had thought were serious at the time were really not serious at all. I felt sincere sadness when I revisited the points in my life where I could have done much better.

Although moving with incredible speed, as though someone had put my life review on superfast forward, I quickly discovered I could linger on any scene that caught my interest, re-experiencing it moment by moment if I desired. My life review was extremely enlightening and continued to be supplemented by a series of scenes that were allegories and parables—a unique teaching experience tailored to my particular needs.

In life, I had been argumentative, especially with my mother. The review revealed clearly how foolish and hurtful all arguments had been. Experiencing others' feelings as well as my own during turbulent episodes was a painful, humbling revelation.

Repentance: the Great Eraser

I was surprised when I realized that wrong deeds for which I had felt remorse and repented of were not in my life review. Those things were gone!

Vividly, however, I realized I *could have repented* for the wrong deeds I was still seeing, such as seeking revenge, being easily provoked, or doing things that worked against my own life's progression.

Most of all, my experience on the Other Side taught me that earth life is a miraculous experience—a time to sow good deeds for glorious heavenly rewards.

Chapter 11

~

A Sphere with No Competition

SUDDENLY, EVERYTHING I HAD learned and seen was surrounding me in this sphere of endlessness. I was aware
again of the presence of the Being of Light and His love
that continued to radiate and powerfully encircle me. I
knew with all my heart that He loved me in spite of the
mistakes I had made in my life. His love was complete, all-
knowing, and unconditional.

A great question then emanated from Him to me so
strongly that it completely penetrated my being. *"In life,
what did you do with what you had?"* Rapidly, the question
engulfed me, commanding an answer.

My Excuses Melt in the Light of Truth

I began answering defensively with reasons and excuses, as
I had in life when I felt I was being called to task for failure
to reach a goal. It was easy to find someone or something to
blame for my failures. I could justify myself with reasons
other than my own shortcomings for my actions, feelings,
or failure to accomplish certain tasks.

I believed my excuses were good reasons to explain why
I hadn't accomplished more: my difficult childhood, others

getting in my way, my poor health, a broken home, my continual strife with my mother, lack of opportunities, and my growing family of children who held me back.

More excuses came welling up within me. If only I had been blessed with strong, supportive parents and raised in an atmosphere of love and acceptance. If I'd had a happy, successful marriage. If only I'd had more money.

I was stopped short in my thinking as I felt all my excuses melting in this Light of Truth. I felt the thoughts and words coming from this Being of Love and Light. *"The question has nothing to do with what you did **not** have in life or with your burdens or faults or problems. But rather, in life, what did you do with what you **did** have?"*

All My Walls of Defense Melted

Oh, the humility and the guilt I felt at that moment. All of my life's actions were seen and known. I couldn't hide them or cover them and my carefully erected walls of excuses that had shielded me from accepting responsibility melted around me. All that was left was just me and the Being of Love and Light who knew everything about me.

I could not rely on or blame anyone else; this question was directed solely at me. I was being measured against no one else—I stood alone, on my own. What did I do with *my* life, with what I *had*, my opportunities, my time on earth? *What had I done with what I **did** have?*

Suddenly I realized that difficulties during earth life were really opportunities. I recognized how problems could be blessings when viewed from the Other Side.

Measured against No One Else

On earth the goal is to win; it is certainly the over-riding desire of sports teams. Winning is the measure of success during earth life; winning means fame and money. Losers are remembered only if the circumstances are humorous, sad, or if the loss is embarrassingly big. The label of

"Loser" is energetically avoided.

Competition is fierce in most aspects of mortal life—from entrance requirements to college to parking spaces at the shopping mall. I was amazed to realize that in the afterlife sphere there is no win or lose, no competition with anyone else. Only *what I did with what I had* mattered. What I did *not* have was irrelevant.

Doing the Best We Can with What We Have

If only I had known to teach my family to do the best they could without the emphasis on winning or losing—to pay attention to how they lived the game of life. Life actually is like a game in a way, but the score that matters is not determined by wins and losses according to the world's standard, but by doing the best we can with what we have.

I now understood that there was no real defeat on earth—only my own choices of attitudes and actions mattered. The important thing was to have kept going, to have looked for solutions, to have striven and endured well until the end of life—to have desired and to have kept trying to live in harmony with Eternal Truths. I realized the need for everyone to help the world be a better place for those living, as well as for future generations.

The Torment of "If Onlys"

In many ways, what I had *not* done with my life seemed more significant than what I *had* done to this point. I knew that every day I had lived on earth I had exchanged a day of my life's time for whatever I had chosen to do that day. Many days I had squandered my fortune of time and now I saw what I had thrown away.

I was very aware that there is eternal joy to be reaped from seeking to do kind deeds and from not being easily offended, on earth and for eternity. I realized that we don't have to be perfect during earth life; just sincerely caring and making an effort to become more loving, charitable, and forgiving—and less judgmental. The desires and intent of the heart are so significant.

Miracles—More than We Know

As I understood earth-life's purpose from an eternal perspective, I became aware that miracles happened abundantly and more easily for those who believed in them. Also, I knew my station or level of life was not as important as the direction I was going, and whether or not I was moving toward eternal goals, appreciating opportunities, and striving to improve.

On the Other Side, I learned that *trying counts*, and all sincere efforts are recognized with accompanying just rewards. My life review showed me with complete clarity that every choice I had made in attitude, thought, or action had an inescapable wanted or unwanted consequence. I alone was responsible for what I had done with my life.

Chapter 12

~

Perspectives from the Other Side

PRIOR TO BEING ON the Other Side, I had not understood reasons for burdens and adversities. It seemed unfair that so many trials and problems brought so much grief during earth life. I wondered why some people have such dreadful lives of hardship and others seem to have relatively few problems. I learned that the answers could not be seen by viewing a short period of time in one's life on earth. But from the perspective of the Other Side, which included everyone's feelings and viewpoint—even the Creator's— everything fits together.

Rich rewards and priceless joy await humble people on earth who valiantly suffer through their trials and tribulations.

Opportunities Are Limitless
Knowledge came to my mind about people who were born with less than I had. I understood that we are not born into equal situations but we all have many more opportunities than we realize. I then knew that many of those who seem to have little according to the world's standards have the opportunity of reaping great rewards on the Other Side.

To Receive Mercy . . .

I learned that adversities are opportunities for personal growth and development and come with built-in benefits that can be enjoyed endlessly. I discovered that justice during earth life is usually found only in the dictionary. Almost everyone on earth is seeking justice, but justice means differing things to different people. What is just to one person is unjust to another. On the Other Side, however, there is complete justice. I recognized how important mercy is and how much more it can be received when it is freely given.

Free-Will Choices and Their Consequences

I understood that God permits us to make our own choices concerning our attitudes, actions, and especially reactions. God does not force us to do what is right during earth life, and we do not have the right to force someone else to do "right" or to make "right decisions;" earth life is a time to learn from choices.

However, I realized that even though God is saddened when we make choices that bring heartache or grief to ourselves or others, He still safeguards our free will to make these decisions. I remembered times during my earth life when I had blamed God for my circumstances and my unhappiness. With this new understanding and perspective, I knew that most of my experiences on earth were the consequences of my choices or my family's choices. Regardless of the difficulties, I could triumph over them with lasting results on the Other Side.

If We Don't Repent . . .

My understanding was opened further as I understood some of the ways repentance works, and that just and terrible consequences may await on the Other Side for those who do not strive to use their earth time wisely and repent of their wrongdoings. When someone intentionally wrongs another, what awaits them is a confrontation of their improper actions and a full realization of their guilt and their lost rewards. However, I discovered that blessings and joy can be received by taking the opportunity to repent and do differently while we are still alive on earth.

Earth life, I found, is designed as a university, a school where we learn from our choices and our mortal experiences. I recognized that my most painful experiences taught me the most. It was enlightening to understand the bigger eternal picture—to know that I was not a victim of circumstances. I learned that I could control my attitude and ultimately, my heavenly rewards.

The Coin Analogy

Suddenly an analogy came to my mind about problems and the difficulty of seeing them from a proper perspective. I wanted to tell my loved ones about a coping technique I'd learned—putting an object the size of a quarter to one eye while closing the other and then to liken that object to a problem. It would be so close that they could only see the problem, or the object. Viewed in this manner, problems can become overwhelming and can conceal obvious solutions.

Next, I envisioned light beginning to appear around the edges of the object as the hand holding it moved slowly away from the eye. Soon the object was far enough away that the things around it could be seen in perspective according to how it fit in and influenced the rest of life. Solutions could now be seen that had been there all the time, but had been concealed, eclipsed by the problem when it was out of perspective.

Every problem has a solution, and God knows that solution. One of the grand and rewarding opportunities of life is to communicate with Him and learn the solutions to our problems. His Light and Truth can flow to us for guidance as we work through problems rather than to give up on them.

Symbolic Parables

Immediately, I recognized this as a visual, symbolic parable of my own life. Problems would have seemed less devastating to me if I had been able to stand back and view each one in its eternal perspective. Answers would have presented themselves. Solutions would have become more obvious.

I realized I *had* grown wiser as a result of my problems and earthly trials. But I saw that I could have gotten through situations, problems, and crises easier and been much further ahead in life, if I had envisioned the end result of my actions instead of staying caught up in the problem.

A Bag Full of Problems

Then I thought of times I had looked at people who seemed problem-free. At times, I had even wished I could trade places with some of them and have the life of peace and ease I mistakenly thought they had.

In the Spirit sphere, a story I'd heard on earth about comparing other people's problems to my own vividly came to my mind. My consciousness was filled with scenes of this visual parable. I saw myself sitting in a roomful of people who were successful and problem-free when measured by worldly standards.

We were passing around a large, dark-colored, expandable bag and all the people were stuffing their problems into it. I could see their trials and challenges that had previously been hidden from my view as they put them into the bag. I realized that if I'd really known these people, I'd have realized that they, too, had problems that seemed as difficult for them as my own did to me. Many of them had even more problems than I did.

As soon as everyone had placed their problems in the bag, it was tossed into the center of the room. The bag popped open and all the problems began spilling out.

Instantly, everyone scrambled to reclaim their own. I dashed in among them, suddenly desperate to find my own set of familiar problems and trials. I did not want anyone else's—only my own.

My Problems Were Tailor-Made Just for Me

I now realized my problems were my own personal, educational building blocks, tailored just for me. Learning from my problems—the cause and effect from my choices, and my parents', and their parents' choices could help me overcome undesired social, cultural, or unwanted family traditions.

Suddenly, I knew I would not want to trade places with anyone else. I needed to grow and develop in my own way, which was different than any other person's way. Someone else's life experiences would not help me to become the individual that I needed to be. I needed my own individualized training.

I now knew that facing challenges builds the "muscles and strengths" of spirit and mind. Only through such *exercises* could I have developed as I needed to do. To build physical muscles, we lift weights. To develop the "muscles" of mind and spirit, we have the chance to solve problems, grow wise through them, and gain skills, knowledge, and talents that remain with us forever.

People Are More Important Than Things

Great truths flooded into my mind. I understood that the more people learned and applied on earth, the more advantage they gain on the Other Side. I realized that when I died, I left behind all material wealth and worldly goods. They didn't really matter anymore—people mattered. I had a vivid awareness of how important people are, especially one's own family.

With new, expanded knowledge, I also knew the importance of learning and developing skills of patience and communication with family and others in earth life; there are endless benefits in the spiritual sphere. I learned that being charitable, patient, and forgiving toward others are some of the most important character traits to be acquired—learned from the school of life.

My perspective had changed completely. These scenes brought me priceless learning experiences, but my learning had just begun.

Chapter 13

∼

Spiritual Muscle Builders
and Coping Techniques

MORE THOUGHTS CAME TO my mind about lessons I'd
learned from troublesome situations. I thought of times I
wanted to stay on a plateau. I heard myself saying, "No
more growth, God, please. Let me just stay where I am.
Please let me rest through a nice coasting period." Instantly,
I realized there's no such thing as coasting—I was either
going forward in life acquiring good habits or I was going
backward acquiring bad habits, such as being impatient or
developing an "I don't care" attitude.

Opportunities for Growth Abound

Returning to scenes from my life review, I was struck with
the realization that daily or routine tasks presented opportunities for strengthening personal characteristics of patience
and understanding for others. Previously, when people did
things I thought were rude—such as crowding in a ticket
line or cutting in front of me in traffic—my desire for justice
surfaced and I felt compelled to verbally express my views to
them, whether they could hear me or not.

I watched many of my actions and *reactions*. Most of the time when I got behind the wheel to drive, I was in a hurry and thought of driving as going from point "A" to point "B." Anything that happened along the way to delay me from my goal aroused my anger.

However, when I observed these scenes from this new perspective, knowing my feelings and also many of the other people's feelings and attitudes, it suddenly seemed foolish and childish to react impulsively and point out others' faults on the highway or anyplace else. I no longer wanted to judge others' motives. I knew the drivers did not realize the full consequences of their actions, as I had not previously, and that impulsive actions could lead to deadly accidents with rippling effects that could cause great anguish.

Angels—the Unknown "Back-Seat Observers"

Driving a vehicle, I saw, was one of many routine tasks that present opportunities to develop good character traits. It was also a definite "mini-test" of character—of how we think, act, and *react* toward others when *it seems no one is watching* or when we think our actions are not really important. Driving in congested traffic can be a great opportunity to build patience.

All situations and challenges, I saw, can be learning experiences. I could have reaped benefits if, when faced with a challenge, I had asked myself, "What can I learn from this situation?" Also, I discovered that it had been a waste of time trying to wish away my challenges, problems, and trials; they were my "spiritual muscle builders."

The Hundred-Year Coping Technique

Coping techniques I could have used in my life became easier for me to understand. I saw that I could have taken a problem or a difficult situation and examined its significance one hundred years from now by asking myself:

Who would have been affected by it, and how? Given that much time, did it still seem major or was it now minor? Taking that problem and sending it one hundred years into the future, how big or how small did it become? Could I even see it? Did it really matter in the outcome of my life? Many of my problems would have shrunk immediately if I had envisioned them by means of that simple technique.

Trials Pass

Life comes in phases, I realized, and each phase seems to stretch out in earth years feeling as if it will last forever— but it never does. *Earth time is not forever.* Situations come and go, and *trials pass.*

I thought again of the young woman and the teenage boy who had committed suicide. If they had waited, things may have improved for them. It was tragic that by not realizing this, they had both taken actions that had forever stopped their earthly growth and regrettably stifled their spiritual life.

We Find What We Look For

My life review continued. I saw that I had received great blessings, more than I knew. I was surprised as I became aware of times my life and my children's lives had been spared, and I realized that everyone on earth has many more blessings and miracles than they recognize at the time.

Repeatedly, I realized that things in my life could have been much worse than they had been. When I was caught up in what went wrong, I overlooked the things that went right and the many blessings I had received.

One fact became clear: *I found what I looked for.* I learned it is better to look for and find things that have gone right—the many blessings received. I saw that by *acknowledging and expressing gratitude for blessings received, even more would be given.* I realized that life and each day had been a gift—if only I had noticed.

The Real Test

Like a light suddenly going on, I understood that if problems could bring blessings and opportunities, then the real test in my life was the intent of my heart and whether or not I had the right attitude. Even in situations that had gone badly for me, I could have passed the test if I'd had good intentions and the right attitude.

It became obvious that there were many times in my life where I had succeeded—such as times I had held my tongue and not argued when someone was verbally venting their frustrations as if I had been the cause of their problem. Joyfully, I was aware of some other times that I had kept good thoughts and intentions when it was extremely difficult to do so.

Life Is Like a Game
With the Score Revealed on the Other Side

I realized that living in the world and accepting the tests throughout life builds character for eternity. Life is somewhat like a game—only the score is actually kept more on the Other Side than on the earth. When my life review showed that there were difficult tests in life I had passed, I was filled with joy.

As knowledge filled my mind, I knew that *each of my adversities carried with it a seed of opportunity* for growth and improvement. But I needed faith to recognize and continue with patience until the growth was realized. That was the challenge—to persist and look for the good.

On the Other Side, the definite realization came to me that I'd had more opportunities than I realized while I was alive and situations could have improved. Then I knew that where I had *been* in earth life was not as important as the *direction* in which I had been going.

Problems Refine the Spirit

Also, I learned that problems can refine the spirit—as I said before, they are spiritual muscle builders. I realized that there are all kinds of coping techniques available on earth if only we open our minds and hearts to them.

But now I believed it was too late for me to utilize the knowledge I gained for earth life. *Being dead was so final!*

Chapter 14

⁓

People Skills Have Eternal Benefits

ON EARTH, MY TREMENDOUS determination to push for fairness and justice in the world led me to have an argumentative attitude.

On the Other Side, knowledge about communications and relationships poured into my consciousness. Scenes from eternity that I was shown seemed personalized for my instruction. Perhaps that is why I was shown many scenes about arguing, its futility, and the damage it causes to relationships

The Futility of Arguments

At one point in my Other Side's view, I saw couples involved in heated disputes shouting at each other. As I watched, I shared their thoughts, feelings, and emotions as they argued. It was almost as though I could step inside each person's mind and heart and know what they were experiencing.

Their Words Did Not Reflect Their Feelings

I was amazed as I observed what was happening: the words each person spoke were completely different from the feelings they had. It was clear that they did not know how to communicate what they felt toward each other or how to explain their feelings without verbally attacking the other person. Obviously they did not understand the other's viewpoint.

Also, what they wanted from their partner was not manifest in what they were saying. In fact, as they argued they strayed far from the original conflict. Their accusations became more outrageous, their demands more and more inappropriate, and they eventually resorted to name calling. However, each partner was feeling hurt and shocked that their loved one's words and responses were as unkind as their own.

One woman was spewing verbal threats at her mate, such as, "If you leave me, I'll take the children so far away you'll never see them again," and, "If you leave, I'll find someone so much better than you." But what she was actually thinking was that she loved her husband and wanted to put her arms around him and calm things for them both; she desperately wanted him to put his arms around her and tell her that he loved her. Not knowing her true feelings, he felt rejected and reacted to her words.

She didn't see that when she hurled angry words at him, she was sowing more anger. As certain as planted seeds yield their own kind, he responded to her hateful words with hateful words of his own—and she was hurt even more. His response was so different from what she wanted that she threw back even more bitter words and threats. The wrangling continued and pointlessly escalated. Their feelings were easy to perceive. They were both bewildered and wondered why the other person hurled back hurtful, vindictive words which surprised and further angered them.

As I shared their feelings, I knew that these arguments and angry emotions grew because of the frustration of not knowing what to say, what to do, or how to respond to the other's behavior. They simply did not know how to express themselves so the other person could understand their viewpoint.

I knew that both the woman and her mate did not even mean the things they were saying; they reacted to what the other was saying without thinking of the consequences. They could not separate themselves from the contention long enough to act the way they wanted to, but trapped themselves in their arguments.

They each felt enormous heartache and emotional pain. I wanted to shout to them, to tell them to stop and listen to what they were saying. If one of them would take time to think about the situation and understand what the other was really feeling, they could have changed everything. If either one of them had stopped criticizing the other and stopped the attacks on the other's most vulnerable points, they could have stopped the argument and avoided irreparable damage to each other's feelings and their relationship.

I learned that most arguments are futile and come from limited understanding of others and from limited communication skills. If a situation could be viewed from all dimensions, including others' perspectives, and if people could control their words, arguments could dwindle or even cease. Sincere empathy and unconditional love would replace the inclination to argue or hurt another.

Opinions Need to Be Listened to—Not Challenged

I understood that things would have been different if any of the people I had seen fighting had simply been strong enough to compassionately look at the other and *quietly listen* and accept their partner's opinions without contradiction. They had their own opinions and were at their own level of growth. They each wanted understanding of their opinion—to be non-judgmentally heard, and to feel loved and accepted. They did not want someone telling them what to do and giving unasked-for solutions.

Each partner needed to see things from the other's point of view without criticizing and giving put-downs. I thought of times I had been in similar situations. The wealth of people skills that had been important and available to me on earth was now vividly apparent in the spiritual realm where I was shown truth.

I became aware of some of the challenges of women involved in arguments because their mates wanted only their own opinion or decision to be accepted as the final word, with no discussion or allowance for expression of a differing viewpoint, opinion, or expansion on their idea. This need caused some women to feel frustrated and to develop pent-up feelings of anger. Other women unleashed harsh words which fueled heated arguments.

Yet I knew relationships on earth could be revitalized if people kept in mind the answer after asking themselves: "How important will this argument be in one hundred years? Even in one hundred days?"

Another couple I saw arguing was, again, one spouse trying to change the other's opinion. I could see that their argument was a waste of time. The more the man bickered and badgered and belittled his wife, the stronger she came back at him with her opinions and accusations. I could feel what she was feeling and I understood why she believed the way she did.

The wife was at a different level of growth than her husband. She thought she was absolutely justified in her beliefs. He, on the other hand, was coming from his level of growth and beliefs. He was feeling greatly frustrated and he could not comprehend why his wife couldn't see his point of view. Childishly, neither person would step back and allow the other to have a different opinion. They didn't even try to see the situation from the other person's viewpoint and neither would let go of their own opinions.

A Coping Technique—Let It Go

I learned an important concept: **Let it go.** I realized there was so much energy wasted in trying to prove oneself right. Arguing over ideas and opinions can ruin relationships. As each person uses words that hurt, it is as if he or she is lighting the fires of anger in the other. Harsh words only add to the other person's anger and they feel more inflamed—it is like trying to put out a fire by throwing on gasoline. Leaving opinions unchallenged can be much wiser.

Watching these couples argue while feeling their real emotions gave me new understandings, patience, and acceptance of others' opinions. It helped me realize how much time I had wasted in contentions and arguments. I became aware that being *unwilling* to see another's viewpoint or not taking time to communicate so *another understands properly* always damages relationships.

The importance and wisdom of listening with an understanding heart and communicating without criticizing and putting others down was impressed upon my mind as I understood the far-reaching consequences and effects of words.

Loving Words Are a Healing Balm

More knowledge came into my mind and I became aware of many benefits of loving unconditionally—especially the importance of *expressing loving words*. I knew that people need to feel loved and to be **told they are loved.** Sincere loving words can be a healing balm to the soul of someone who is hurting.

Thoughts came to my mind of some of the many times in my life when I had yearned to feel loved. I knew that I was not alone. Usually women, even more than men, long to hear those precious words, "I love you."

I wondered why it was so difficult for most men to understand women's feelings; why it was usually difficult for them to express loving words. With that thought, it was as though I could see through a man's eyes and feel with a man's heart. I suddenly knew how different men's perspectives are from women's and that women can be extremely difficult for them to understand. With this new awareness, I realized how difficult it is for most men to express their feelings and emotions, and that generally, it is easier and more natural for women to talk about what bothers them.

Men usually don't know what a woman means when she says she doesn't *feel* loved, or when she wants to discuss all the things that upset her. Men usually believe they are *showing* love by working hard for their families, and they often think that loving words are unnecessary. Usually the man does not know how to respond and may withdraw— the opposite response the woman wants.

I realized that some of this lack came from the example of parents who did not express their feelings—traditions handed down from generation to generation. Also, the sexes were created with definite differences in temperaments and emotions for many good reasons. However, I knew that situations and people could change as they react and adapt to each other's differences.

Arguments Have No "Victor"

From these scenes I viewed on the Other Side, I became aware that quarreling over differences does not lead to solutions, and arguments are never actually "won." If a "victory" hurts another there is no real victory. The couples I saw arguing did not have clear goals; arguing had become a habit and was destructive to the self-esteem of those involved— especially to the tender feelings of children.

The people in these arguments did not realize that they displayed their own faults when they raised their voices for emphasis, shouted, and used profanity to make an impression. It was observable that they were without adequate words in their vocabulary and that they were trying to sound smarter, more "right," speaking in this manner.

Being unwilling or unable to communicate effectively, they shouted put-downs.

At times they laughed at others or became angry or labeled them "stupid" for not agreeing with their opinions or for not following their instructions. They did not see that the failing was their own—they were not communicating adequately.

Watching these couples locked in useless arguing and knowing the feelings of each partner, I became aware that people skills—especially communication skills—are a vital part of the mortal experience. Whether or not we choose to learn them will have far-reaching effects.

Chapter 15

∽

How to Gain Mercy—Not Justice!

IN MY LIFE REVIEW, I saw times where I had been offended or hurt by someone and also times when I had been the one causing an offense. I watched the way I acted or reacted. I experienced the same thoughts and felt the feelings I had at those moments, and I knew the thoughts and experienced the feelings of other individuals involved. This gave me a new profound awakening and awareness of my senses, and my consciousness was filled with understanding of our motivations. At the time I had misjudged others because I did not know *their* viewpoints. I regretted making a big issue of seeking justice. I had wanted those who seemed to deliberately hurt others, to "pay" for their behavior.

I was critical and would get upset when people who appeared cruel or unfair to others would prosper from their ruthlessness. I thought that they did not have many trials or tribulations, but led happy lives. In contrast, I wondered why many humble, kind people seemed to trudge through life having to bear numerous hardships and trials.

Things Are Infinitely Fair on the Other Side

When my awareness was expanded to view situations in their proper eternal perspective, *I knew that after someone had lived his or her life and gone to the Other Side, they would face their actions, and no one would get ahead unfairly.* Good deeds, small and large, would be rewarded and bad ones would reap punishment.

Gathering Good Deeds for Other-Side Enjoyment

I realized that earth time had been my time for gathering kind thoughts, deeds, and actions for enjoyment on the Other Side. I wish I could adequately describe the feelings I felt, the sorrow I experienced to have criticized or misjudged another of God's children in any way during my journey through life. In instances where I'd hurt another's feelings, I felt deep remorse.

Also, I knew that if someone hurts another and seems to get away with it, as if robbing justice while alive on earth, there was no need wishing revenge on them. If someone does not seem to have a conscience on earth, it does not mean that they do not have one; they do and it will pain them with an agony later. They are really hurting themselves.

As We Judge, So Shall We Be Judged

However, instead of being relieved or grateful that others would someday have to pay for their behavior, I felt sorrow for them as I realized that they were losing their other-side rewards and bringing punishment on themselves. With my new and increased understanding of eternal rewards and eternal punishments, I no longer wanted revenge or retaliation against anyone for anything. I knew that it was a Great Universal Truth that what we give out comes back to us. As we judge others we will be judged. As we sow, so shall we reap.

Forgive to Be Forgiven

I knew that if I wanted to receive mercy, I needed to give mercy while I was alive. I wanted to be able to forgive anyone and everyone who had offended me. I discovered that it was literally true that we earn what we receive on the Other Side by the choices we make while on the earth. As I experienced my life review and understood things in their proper perspective, I saw that each time I had wished justice on another I was determining the way I would judge myself.

Glorious Feelings Come from Being Kind

Then the thought forcefully came to my mind that if what I give out is truly what I get back, I didn't want justice, I wanted mercy! I knew that if I wanted to receive mercy, I would had to have given mercy while I was alive. I wanted to return to earth life and be merciful to others. Also, I knew that if I had intentionally offended one of God's children, it was an offense to God.

I knew for myself what I had done or not done on earth and glorious feelings of joy accompanied the good I had done, especially for those who seemed to deserve it least.

God Loves All Creatures

More knowledge came to my mind with a sharp awareness of truth about the importance of being kind and merciful not only to people, but to all of God's creatures: animals, birds, reptiles, etc. God's love extends to His creatures in all their wondrous variety and so should ours. I knew that they were placed on earth for wise purposes and that they are not to be intentionally mistreated.

All of the knowledge I had been shown added to my understanding of the importance of the time on earth and the joy I could have reaped if I had spent more of my time giving mercy rather than seeking justice. *The heavenly rewards that can be earned are worth the effort!*

This truth touched my soul and gave great meaning to the Biblical teaching, "But glory, honour, and peace, to every man that worketh good…" (Romans 2:10)

Chapter 16

~

A Source of Joy beyond Comprehension

ABRUPTLY, I WAS AGAIN aware of the question from the Being of Light. As He repeated it to me, it pierced my consciousness. He asked, "What did you do with what you had in life?" This question had nothing to do with blessings other people received in their lives, or what others had done with their circumstances in life. Rather, I absolutely knew again that I was not competing against anyone else's good works; there was no one else to blame for my omissions. He was asking me only what I did with what I *did* have. My sins of omission became very obvious to me—there were things I did *not* do that I should have done with what I was given, such as being more charitable, patient, and helpful to others.

My chance at mortal life's opportunities to grow mentally and spiritually was finished. I wanted to run, to hide—anything to not have to face the reality that I'd not done what I could have during my earth life. But I knew that my own thoughts and actions had earned what I was experiencing.

Unconditional Love — a Source of Peace

Then I thought of some of the little good deeds I had done for others that only they and I knew, such as when I took time to cheer and visit someone who needed encouragement, especially when it was not convenient. These were things that I thought to be insignificant at the time.

However, in the Spiritual realm, I was benefitting from small acts of kindness in a much larger way. The joy I received from my little kind deeds was magnified and I realized that God was pleased when one of His children helps another one. Precious feelings of joy flooded over me and I knew that *all* compassionate acts of charity and kindness, *even small ones*, reap joy and great rewards. Also, I understood the importance of true, unconditional love for others. Every word or action motivated by love, not because someone did something for me first, brought peace to my soul.

I knew God had set the example for us by loving every one of us unconditionally. As I thought of this, my being was infused again with total love from the God of Love and Light. I felt love radiate from Him all through and around me. God's love was so magnificent that it vastly expanded my feelings of love and empathy for others. I marveled that I could feel that deeply, that *anyone* could feel that much love.

As more knowledge expanded my consciousness, it became clear that a higher way of living could be accomplished on earth. It required constant choices to avoid condemning, gossiping, criticizing, and judging others.

Even though it would be a continual day-to-day challenge for most everyone, I knew there would be more lasting happiness while living on earth for those who strive to avoid judging others. Family traditions and personal traits of being loving and forgiving could be handed down to posterity by example and all could reap eternal rewards.

Accepting Differences Brings Freedom

I became aware that appreciating others and their differences promotes creativity and diversity and enjoyment. It became clear there are differences in people's likes and their actions according to their age, experience, and family influence. I knew it would be sad if we all had the same likes and dislikes; things would look dull if everyone wanted the same color and kind of cars, houses, or clothes. Suddenly I knew that diversity makes the world an interesting and colorful place.

Learning from Choices

Then I knew that accepting people at their own level of growth and patiently letting them learn from their choices can bring peace and joy beyond description. Acceptance would bring a form of freedom—freedom from pettiness, from prejudice, from judging and being judged. The freedom I felt was wonderful as I understood that each person has different interests and goals and was to be permitted to learn from the results of their choices.

More knowledge came to my mind that there are immeasurable benefits for not judging people's actions, looks, or differences. I understood that when people felt accepted and were permitted to make their free-will choices, they could more easily grow to their personal potential.

At this point, I was understanding things from the perspective of eternal growth, viewing all phases of a situation, all sides, along with the feelings of those involved. I could see the results, the repercussions of my wrongful decisions or indecisions.

The Truth and Beauty of the Scriptures

My thoughts turned to the scriptures and I was impressed with their truthfulness, beauty, and the rewards to be gained by learning and striving to live God's teachings. I was amazed to realize how literally true and wise the scriptures are. I knew that just reading their words could never do them justice, but by pondering them also, more of their meaning could be recognized.

We Cannot Fool God or Ourselves

My every action or reaction, I found, went out in time like unending circles that somehow came back to me. Anything I did or did not do for anyone else had an effect that came back to me. I could no more fool God into thinking I had done my best with my time on earth than I could fool myself.

I Wanted to Shout from the Housetops

Wanting to return to my body on earth to apply what I had learned, I wanted desperately to be able to speak. I felt that if I were given the chance to tell others, I would shout from the rooftops what I had learned: *the importance of being forgiving and the countless blessings that can be reaped by being kind, merciful, and by loving unconditionally.*

Still, I believed my plea was in vain. I had made my choice. The saddest experience I ever had was to recognize all the things I could *no longer do* and to know that I could not make any corrections to my choices. I was racked with torment as I realized that I could no longer even attempt to repent and do better in life.

Forgiving for My Sake

On earth, I had taken classes that taught a *false* process for getting over offenses: First, tell those involved how much they had hurt me. Second, talk it out. Third, receive an apology from the offender(s) and fourth, let it go. Mistakenly, however, I was told I was to receive an apology from the offender before I moved on.

When my knowledge was expanded, to my surprise I discovered I was not to tell someone how I felt about them and then forgive them. I was to forgive others unconditionally and treat others as I would want to be treated, not just for their sake, but for *mine*, because of how I would feel about myself and my actions. Forgiving, forgetting, and letting go of grudges brings benefits for all concerned, whether offenders apologize and ask for forgiveness or not.

Knowing that the sooner I rid myself of feeling offended, the better off I would be. I saw that I could have gained peace of mind in the mortal world and had more peace in the Spiritual realm if I'd done this. I knew that anger at *anyone* hurt me mentally, physically, and especially spiritually.

Even though there was a different sense of "time" on the Other Side, I realized I had learned a lot and had seen many scenes since my transition from earth life to the Spirit World. At that time, I thought that I might be caught endlessly in this awful state where I was filled with feelings of remorse.

Forgive before It's Too Late

Suddenly, I felt myself moving through a space of dense blackness and through the midst of miserable souls who had died while still holding onto angry, bitter grudges toward others. They carried their dark, angry feelings with them in the Spirit realm, and they could not let go of them. Wanting to escape the angry feelings, I found myself floating away from the darkness and through space. Coming down through a beam of light, I found myself looking into a room in a hospital. I saw an older man lying in a hospital bed blankly staring toward the end of his bed and upward toward the ceiling.

I wondered if he could see me looking down on him, but then I knew he could not. Drifting into and out of consciousness, he was too weak to move or communicate with the man and woman standing at the side of his bed. By mental communication, I knew that the woman about his same age was his wife, and the younger man was his son.

Also I realized that the father had been very angry with his son and had not spoken to him for years, except with extremely harsh words. The mother and son felt that his bad feelings had added to the deterioration of the father's health. The son had avoided further contact; each believed the other should apologize. Now, with the father's impending death, there was great sadness displayed on the faces and in the words of the mother and son. The son had tears rolling down his cheeks and his voice broke as he said, "Dad, I'm so sorry for hurting you. Please forgive me; I love you. Please forgive me, Dad." He repeated the words many times, as he cried and asked for forgiveness.

I understood the son's sorrow. He knew it was too late; his father was dying and could not respond. But the young man continued trying to make himself heard and to apologize. It was easy to observe that the young man felt tremendous guilt knowing he had waited too long to speak the precious words his father wanted to hear but that he could not previously bring himself to say, "I am sorry. I love you."

The son turned toward his mother and tearfully said, "Mom, I am so sorry for not apologizing to Dad before. I know I have hurt us all. I am sorry I wasn't there when Dad needed me." He turned back to his father and continued crying and apologizing but still with no response from the father.

The mother lowered her head as she softly cried, too. I understood her pained emotions; she felt torn between her son and husband, and she had lost the enjoyment of them both over this family feud. Her sadness was intensified now, for the two of them and for herself.

Watching them, I wondered how long this young man would feel these terrible feelings of remorse. I did not receive an answer, but I recognized many of my own foolish feelings when I had been involved in futile arguments and waited for another person to apologize. I now recognized the value of putting a relationship ahead of receiving words of apology.

"Time" Is Too Limited to Hold Grudges

Many people, I now knew, feel offended and wait for the other to take the first step in the forgiving process—to call and say they are sorry. They wait to hear those most price-less words, "I love you." But when they are close to death they have painful feelings of wanting to be able to com-municate their love. I knew that when they were finally facing death, they no longer wanted to express anger, but rather, they wanted to ask for forgiveness, express love, and feel the other's love in return.

No one on earth knows for sure when their time may unexpectedly run out, when it will be too late to communi-cate their love. I thought of my own circumstances and I knew that time is too limited to waste holding grudges, being angry, and withholding love.

Forgiveness Brings Glorious Freedom

We take our feelings with us when we die. Those who are patient with others, who are able to forgive when feeling offended and let go of anger on earth, experience great feelings of glorious freedom and inner peace on the Other Side. They reap joy beyond comprehension.

When my understanding was opened, I sincerely sor-rowed for those who hold grudges, intentionally hurt another's feelings, or try to take advantage of others. They would not do or say hurtful things if they realized the seemingly unending ripples of repercussions from regret-table actions. Decisions to hurt others result in lost oppor-tunities for reaping joy and eternal peace of mind.

Chapter 17

~

The Truth That Brings Self-Worth
and Personal Power

THROUGHOUT MY LIFE I had struggled to feel confident. I had not been happy with my weight or my appearance. Most of my life I felt I was too heavy or too old or too ill. When I looked in the mirror, my attention focused on my physical imperfections.

On the Other Side, I gained an entirely different impression of my body. When I watched my life review, it became clear what a valuable gift my body was and how necessary it was to accomplish what I desired to do during earth life. I didn't need to be unhappy because I did not look a certain way or was not the same size as someone else. The important thing was that I *had* a body. It had been dependent on how I treated it; if I had kept it healthy it could have served me well rather than hindered my progress during my life's journey.

In the spiritual realm, I realized how my own poor health habits (such as not eating properly, not getting enough rest or exercise, or pushing myself to the point of exhaustion) had impacted my health and body.

Too late I learned that my body was precious and

vitally important for many reasons and that without it I could not even pick up a piece of paper. My earthly body had many limitations, many ailments, and had caused me much pain, but I had not realized it gave me freedom as well—the freedom to act, to do the things I chose to do, and to participate in earthly experiences.

Unfinished Business

I anguished about important things I wanted to return to earth to do or finish that I could only accomplish with a body. While I was alive on earth I had been unhappy about what I could not do that I had believed my body would not let me do. I had more patience for someone else's physical limitations than my own.

On the Other Side, I saw the importance of prioritizing time and tasks in order to accomplish more and still have energy left for the next day. While I was alive on earth, I did not like wasting time and it seemed nonproductive to rest when there was so much to be done. If I had only realized the truth about health, taking care of the body, and the wise use of time, including resting when needed, I could have enjoyed my journey through life with better health.

I became aware that there is an *energy-force reserve* available to draw from during life on earth. When I made withdrawals from the reservoir of energy I needed to put life-giving things back into it by eating the right foods, maintaining a good mental attitude, taking care of relationships by doing things for others. These were important keys to keep the body's energy reserves filled and make possible earthly enjoyment and heavenly rewards.

Feeling Chained to Circumstances

During my earth life, I had taken self-improvement classes, but I still needed more confidence. There were times I believed my timid feelings and attitudes helplessly chained me to my circumstances.

As I relived these feelings, suddenly a scene was presented to my view that was symbolic of what I had thought about and how I had felt. I saw myself lying on a bright, sandy beach flat on my back. Heavy chains across my limbs bound me tightly and held me firmly against the hot sand. Lifting my head, I could see that the oppressive chains were too strong for me to escape.

As I examined them, I realized and understood what they really were—my own feelings of inadequacy. They were all the put-downs from other people, my own negative self-talk, my painful feelings of incompetence, and perceived lack of abilities.

The Freedom of Truth

The chains held me so that I was hardly able to move. I wondered how I had been able to function in my life with such strong chains binding me. The situation seemed hopeless, and I felt completely unable to help myself.

Just when I was about to give in to complete despair, I felt an infusion of love from God. My mind opened to the knowledge of my true nature; I was not just another life form, *I was a child of God.*

True Empowerment Comes from God

My thoughts centered on that incredible Being of Love and Light who stood by my side. Feelings of empowerment, self-worth, confidence, and the unconquerable courage to be myself immediately filled my being. My inferiority complex was gone. All negative thoughts suddenly disappeared, replaced with my new awareness of reality.

The limits I had put on myself came to mind, and I knew that in earth life I did not need to be chained down with feelings of inadequacy. My self-worth was not dependent on other people. I was important to God, was one of His creations, and I knew He loved me. I realized that God is no respecter of fame or fortune. *Everyone is important to Him—and to themselves.*

This view and understanding filled me with gratitude and a feeling of being loved. Then I sensed a feeling of freedom. In that state of mind I moved my arm; I saw that it came up freely. Amazed, I turned to look at my other arm; it was free also. The chains I had thought were so strong were actually insubstantial and powerless to hold me. Kicking my legs, I found them free as well, and now I was completely free!

Standing, I turned and looked back at the sand where I had lain so hopelessly bound just a few moments before. The chains of self-doubt had melted; they were gone. How could this be? The chains that had hampered me all my life had lacked substance and truth. No one had unlocked them, no one pulled them away from me, yet they now had no power over me. Only one thing made the difference between freedom and captivity: knowledge of my importance to God and to myself.

Dispelling False Beliefs Brings Personal Power

No person had unlocked my chains because no other person had the power to do so. The only power they had ever had was the power of my belief in them. They had seemed and felt so real, but they were *not* real—they were of my own making. They were a hoax, a trick I had played on myself. But no mental chains were strong enough to bind me when I realized that I was a child of God and had great personal power.

Although I didn't realize it, I always had the power to stand and walk away from my chains of self-doubt and low self-esteem. I had within me the power to dispel the dark untruths I had believed about myself throughout my life. The knowledge of my true nature turned on the light in my inner self and illuminated my path to freedom.

When I thought back on the many books I had read and courses I had taken that I had thought were fantastic, now they all seemed trivial. All the books and courses in the world were nothing when compared with the knowledge and confidence I gained when I actually realized *I was a child of God.*

Programming the Computer of the Mind

While on the Other Side, I learned that the mind was like a powerful computer that needed to be constantly cared for with proper input. Otherwise, the product it produced would be of poor quality—and that product is *who* we are.

Vividly I realized how important it was to avoid self-disparaging thoughts that would produce unwanted results. Such thoughts when allowed to stay in my mind had formed the chains that pulled me down and hindered my growth.

I realized that my mind was powerful, but it was also my servant, a part of my earthly body given me to use wisely; I was in charge. I could have taken command of my thinking and my attitudes. I could have worked at keeping my mind on things I wanted instead of on things I worried about. On earth, I could have re-programmed my thinking—because I was a child of God.

Self-worth and personal power, I learned, are **not** a result of looking or acting a certain way or achieving a certain amount. They come from knowing and remembering the truth: *I am a child of God.*

Chapter 18

~

Scenes of Premortality

SUDDENLY, THE SCENES IN my life review were gone and scenes of my premortal life came into view. I was aware that I was part of a large group of enthusiastic supporters of the planned earth life. Immediately I knew I was not born on earth simply by chance. There were reasons—eternal purposes for everything. I knew about the earth's creation and had a great love for it.

Everything was designed to fit together and function in harmony, and I observed that each part has a reason for being; each part supports all other parts by its existence—even insects. Things I had taken for granted or thought of as insignificant now had new importance. All things, I now knew, are significant and necessary to help the earth be whole and complete.

For example, water—an everyday substance—is important in every aspect of life on earth. Next, I knew the importance of trees that purify the air, filtering it and creating oxygen. I was never fond of trees and vegetation before. My favorite landscaping would have been almost exclusively rocks.

That changed when I knew how important trees are

and how dependent everything is on everything else. Trees, vegetation, and seeds took on a new significance for me. How gloriously everything functioned; how marvelously it was created! I had a new respect and appreciation for all of God's creations. The love I had for earth was tremendous. It was incredibly important to me as I realized the significance of it in the plan and miracle of creation.

In the premortal world, I saw that it was earth life that would allow me the opportunity to have a mortal body and mortal experiences. My understanding increased as I realized why our memories of premortal life have to be hidden with an earthly veil of forgetfulness: *so that we can **gain wisdom**—learn, develop mentally and spiritually, find joy through obedience, and become more loving, charitable, and forgiving.* Also, I realized that I could not have functioned properly on earth if I had remembered the joy of being engulfed in Godly love. The longing would have been so great to be back in His presence that I could not have withstood the pain.

I Chose to Come to Earth

When I was on the Other Side, I wondered about life before birth, and whether I had wanted to be born or had any choice about it. My question was answered profoundly in these quick glimpses of premortality. I distinctly remembered with a burst of happiness some of the excitement I had felt about coming to earth. I knew I was not alone in this excitement; all of us were eager to participate in this plan. We were not *lukewarm* about this; we were exuberant. With this realization and refreshing of my memory, I felt repentant for having wondered whether I had wanted to be born—the answer was so obviously **yes.**

Each of Us Has a Purpose

My remembrance of the premortal world while on the Other Side reawakened my feelings and knowledge about the wonders connected to being born, having a body, and being part of this eternal plan. With a bright awareness, I recalled that I wanted to help make the earth a better place for those who would come after me and be part of the whole.

My birth on earth was for a purpose which I accepted and wanted to accomplish. I wanted to be part of the group who were creating benefits for others in the world. I knew that each choice made on earth can have far-reaching effects. Every person and every choice matters more than we can realize at the time.

I was amazed at what I was shown and what I learned from glimpses of premortal life, scenes of the spirit world, and revelations of knowledge that were impressed upon my consciousness. The events in premortality and earth life only fit together when viewed from life on the Other Side.

The additional knowledge was given to me that the earth is for all of God's children, and the responsibility for it belongs to all of us. However, there are many who come to earth who do not realize or care about its importance. Knowing that the earth was being fouled by some for whom it was created, whose lives depended on it, caused me to feel great sadness.

Every Person and Every Creature Matters to God

It was painful to observe those who mistreat other people under their care, including helpless children and the elderly. Their pain when confronted with their own actions will be worse than that which they inflicted.

Thoughts came to my mind of those who regrettably discount the intelligence, emotions, and feelings of pain of animals—and any creatures on earth—sometimes because they didn't care and sometimes because they did not realize the eternal nature of God's creations. I knew that many people on earth greatly underestimate how much God cares about His animals and other creatures and how people treat them. It was sad that many who had high possibilities fell short of their potential in their treatment of their families, others, and defenseless creatures.

It was exciting, however, to learn of the tremendous joy awaiting those who accept their challenges and make it through them while striving to keep God's commandments—they then reap their *earned* rewards. I had an overwhelming desire to be among the group on earth who serve Him and do His will.

However, many of my own free-will choices while I was alive on earth had brought me feelings of remorse instead.

Chapter 19

≈

Eternal Perspectives

My life review continued and my attention focused on scenes with my mother. I became aware of thoughts I'd had on earth such as, "Why didn't I have someone else as my mother or my father?" I heard my thoughts: "My life would have been so much better if I had had different parents. I could have accomplished so much more." It was as though those thoughts were visible around me. I tried to escape from them, but I could not.

Just as suddenly, other things were in my view and I knew that I had chosen my mother although I wasn't told this was the case for everyone else. I had *wanted* to be her daughter, not for the things she could do for me on earth, but for what I could do for her. She needed me! She was a special, precious person who needed my help to make it through her journey of earth life. In her own way, she was hurting as much as I had been.

I Was Wrong about Being Right

Our lives together had been filled with contention and arguments over what was truth and who was right. We had often used words that hurt each other and our relationship had been extremely frustrating for both of us. It seemed we were always angry with each other.

For years I had longed to hear her tell me she loved me and that she was sorry about my unhappy childhood. I wanted her to accept me but I felt I could never please her. We argued over big things and little things. A poem came to mind that I had written when I was a teenager expressing my mistaken feelings about being right. The poem reads:

> *Oh Mother dear, I sadly fear*
> *that until we die*
> *we will continue to try*
> *to argue and fight*
> *to prove who is right*
> *although we both know, I am.*

Erroneously, I had believed that finding out who was "right" would cure almost any situation. I had falsely believed that a vigorous pursuit of justice in all things was essential, as if it would automatically stop wrongful actions as soon as "truth" was discovered. The stark reality of how false this notion was became clear to me. I discovered how wrong I was to quarrel about being right and saw that everyone believes, or likes to think they're right.

Who was right or wrong, whether she was sorry or not, or whether she told me she loved me was no longer a concern. Oh, how my feelings for my mother and my understanding of her changed. No longer did I feel compelled to have her say or do something to show she loved me. I knew of her love for me. I *felt* her feelings as though I had been her.

My Mother Needed Me

My awareness exploded with the information and reality of how much my mother needed me. My love for her blossomed and I realized her heartaches and life's trials. I missed her in this spiritual sphere and I wanted to help her and talk to her; I was saddened and frustrated that I could not. As I realized this, my feelings of remorse intensified. I had let us both down. Also, I knew that she had a difficult time telling me she loved me and she needed me to tell her I loved her.

The foolishness and futility of bickering and fighting with *anyone* was impressed upon me. I was very sorry for wasting irreplaceable time senselessly arguing about happenings, situations, opinions, and who was right. My sorrow was extreme for every harsh or sharp word I had ever spoken to anyone, especially family members.

We Learn from Each Other

Also, I saw that people watch and learn from each other and repeat each other's actions and mistakes. It became clear to me how everyone's *actions* influence the basic lives of countless others

Quickly, new scenes came to my view containing additional, important messages for me. I saw a mother teaching her daughter to clean a floor thoroughly. Her voice was sweet as she approvingly said, "The floor looks nice and clean, but that corner could look better and needs to be redone." The mother's words conveyed her love and acceptance and did not make the girl feel rejected but motivated her to improve her skills. I understood that the mother's object was not only to get the floor clean, but to instill confidence in her child and to teach her good work habits for life.

Again, the scene before me changed swiftly and I saw another mother belittling her child for not doing the chores according to *her* standards. The mother grabbed the cleaning cloth from her daughter and said in a sharp tone of voice, "Why do I have to do everything myself? You are so clumsy, you can't do anything right." Then she did the task herself. I saw the young child cringe as she developed habitual feelings of inferiority and depression that would lead her toward giving up.

I became aware that the ultimate goal in teaching children is to help them learn and mature so that they can succeed without being supervised. They need a safe family environment in order to gain wisdom, confidence, and the experience of doing things on their own. They need an *inner* desire to do things correctly, not because they are being watched or because someone makes them perform their tasks to an acceptable standard.

Entrusted to My Care

This was an enlightening revelation for me. I wanted to cry out to my children—to apologize for the times I was impatient with them as they went through their learning experiences during childhood. Then I also knew that my children were actually *God's* children entrusted to my care. From this perspective, I understood that problems as I was raising them were really opportunities for us to learn some of life's valuable lessons, such as the connection between choices and consequences.

I had always loved my children, but now I had gained a vivid new understanding of how extremely important and precious they were. Also, I missed them in this sphere and I longed to be able to talk to them. I wanted to tell them about things they could do on earth that would help them prepare for their journey to the Other Side.

Teaching Opportunities Are Fleeting

Rapidly, scenes from priceless child-rearing years passed for my review. The swift passage of the time I had with my children brought the distinct realization that my best opportunities for teaching them were gone—in fact *all* opportunities to be with them or to teach them on earth were *gone*.

When I was alive on earth, I had seen a wall plaque

with a saying on it, "Life was what happened while I was busy with other plans." I was struck in this spiritual realm with the actuality of that statement. Before I realized it, those brief childhood times while my children's questioning minds were so open and accepting of ideas had passed, never to be recaptured.

I looked back over the years when my children were small with their minds absorbing my philosophies and attitudes as they matured. I heard words I had said many times as they were growing up, and winced: "Who's at fault? Tell the truth—what happened here? We have to be fair about this. You are wrong."

Those parenting phrases seemed normal; they were ones I often heard in my own childhood and so repeated as a parent. I wanted to raise my children to seek fairness and justice. That was how I had been raised and how my mother had been raised.

The scenes I viewed while I was on the Other Side revealed to me the error of seeking "truth" and "fairness" over teaching forgiveness and tolerance. Being right or establishing fault faded into insignificance compared to being concerned about feelings, building character, and developing self-esteem while children are young and most open to training.

Words Can Hurt

As quickly as my mind comprehended these scenes, my vision expanded to the view of many little children. I felt the feelings of these small children as they took harsh verbal attacks from parents locked into patterns of false child-rearing notions that went back several generations (including put-downs and words that battered self-images, words that could hurt like a blow from a fist).

I saw parents yelling at their children, who in frustration and anger falsely believed they were reacting normally to their situations. The children absorbed like little sponges the tone of their parent's voices and the tensions around them. Like little tape recorders, they were recording in their minds the words they heard their parents use.

Mental Tape Recorders

Then I saw those same children as adults with their children. It was as though someone hit the playback button on their mental tape recorders. They were using their parents' impatient and ineffective responses word for word. They were parenting the way they had been taught, following their parents' unsuccessful example.

My children came into my view and I knew how precious and important they were as part of my life. Each child had been like a jewel I was given on earth to care for, lovingly polish, and help develop its special radiance. I loved them very much and wanted to communicate with them. My love and concern for them was infinitely more than it was while I was with them in earth life. I had no idea the "spiritual sphere" was this way. I wanted to go back to earth to warn them not to repeat the mistakes I had made.

Suddenly my feelings of remorse in regard to my lack of parenting skills ceased. Wait! I thought defensively, I had not been given an "owner's manual" when I had my first child, nor had my mother. I was doing the best I knew how, and so had my mother and her parents. We believed we were doing right at the time. In reality, we were functioning at our own level of growth, just as everyone does.

Excuses Melt in the Bright Light of Truth

I also realized that people can break free of undesirable teachings and habits, including undesired family traditions. It is not easy, yet it can be done with the help of the Creator through the power of prayer and a person's own self-determination. My excuses continued to melt in the bright light of truth.

The perspectives I gained about all the members of my family cast a new light of understanding on the importance of every pattern handed down from one generation to another. I wanted to change many of the ones that were being handed down to my posterity—but now I could not.

Chapter 20

✑

Mingling with Angels

As SOON AS I grasped the meaning of these scenes, I found myself quickly traveling through time and space through a star-filled blackness. Suddenly, I stopped. I clearly saw parenting patterns being passed downward from my children, to theirs, and onward. Also, I saw generations of people from many lands and cultures continuing with family experiences and traditions, good or bad.

The Being of Love and Light was just a short distance from me and was showing me the spirits of many people whom I somehow knew were several generations of *my* posterity.

Then I saw a beautiful young woman with lovely dark hair and beautiful blue eyes. I couldn't stop staring at her; I felt drawn to her. As our eyes met, she smiled and held out her arms toward me. But she paused and with her arms still outstretched she said, "I've waited so long." Putting her arms down, she then turned and was gone. Years later I learned who the girl was, as demonstrated by the following occurrence:

In 1993, Jessica, my great-granddaughter, was just a little toddler about two years old the first time I saw her. As I came out of the airport terminal door, I saw her with her mother, Crystal. She ran up to me with her arms outstretched in such a familiar way, just as the young woman I had seen on the Other Side. And this tiny child said the same thing I'd heard her say then: "I've waited so long."

As she said those words and as we hugged, I felt spirit-to-spirit and heart to heart. I knew she was the same beautiful young woman I had seen on the Other Side.

Later, Crystal told me that little Jessica normally never spoke like that, nor did she ever talk like that again.

Now, about 21 years later, Jessica has two little boys, my great-great grandsons. We had our five-generation picture taken at my 80th birthday party, given by my daughter, Patty Taylor, November 2, 2013.

In this picture I am surrounded by my daughter Suzan Walker, Crystal Conklin (my granddaughter), Jessica Royston (my great-granddaughter), and Kaiden and Brentley Royston (my two great-great-grandsons).

In 1983, while I was on the Other Side in the Spirit World, I was among many adult spirits and mingling with angels. They were all around me and as I passed through their midst I had a deep understanding that many of them would be my posterity on earth.

Family Is More Important than Success

I was struck with the knowledge of how important the family and home life are—more important than anything else. Any other success is temporary. I knew that gaining all the success the world has to offer is meaningless compared to the family.

Even though I had been away from my family largely because of poor health, I knew we could have spent more quality time together. If I had been able to set a better example for them by being more empathetic, loving, and nurturing, rather than seeking "fairness" to settle sibling disputes, it would have strengthened family relationships.

With this awareness, as I looked at all these precious ones, I wanted to hide from them. I didn't want to admit who I was or that part of the problems they would have on earth stemmed from me and what I had or had not done. I knew now that all actions, large and small, good or bad, have eternal consequences.

As soon as I had that thought, I recalled Crystal, my granddaughter, sitting quietly at my home and playing a silly game that had occupied much of her free time. I re-heard the soft "Ping, Ping, Ping" when she had scored points as she played the game over and over. Her concentration had been intense. I had a burning feeling that there were other things she needed to do and learn, things that would help her in her mortal development.

Spending so much time playing that unproductive game was creating a void in her development. Instead, she should be learning things she could pass on to her posterity. She had waited a long time for her opportunity to have a mortal body and her precious time was being squandered in front of a video screen I had purchased for her and taught her how to use. I wanted to return to earth life and hide that game.

Looking at my posterity all around me, I sadly realized that my lack of child-rearing skills would contribute to some of the unhappiness they would have when they went to earth. Challenges resulting from my inadequacy would ricochet through time. I knew of some of the trials they would go through in their lives; troubles caused by knowledge they lacked because I didn't teach my children, and they in turn didn't teach theirs, and so on.

There were things they would not learn on earth which would have greatly benefitted them. I saw that my future posterity could trace this lack of knowledge for generations, back to my children, to me, to my mother, and to my ancestors. During my earth life, I had never thought of these things, but in the spirit world, they were apparent.

My anguish intensified as I understood the far-reaching effects of not helping my granddaughter learn more worthwhile things. Crystal was losing precious growing experiences that would mean some lost eternal rewards that she may have otherwise gained as she taught her posterity, *my* posterity.

Gaining Wisdom, a Grand Key to Happiness

I saw that gaining wisdom and overcoming problems are some of the grand keys God gives us to unlock our own happiness and the growth and happiness of our posterity and those around us. I saw how loving parenting skills would help all concerned. Also, I realized the importance of believing that situations and relationships can improve and then working to better things rather than being quick to judge and give up on a family member.

As I mingled with angels and those whom I knew were to be my posterity, my understanding was opened and I

knew that these parenting skills were some of the important lessons that were to be learned in the school of life.

～

Chapter 21

Fads and Fashions—Whirling through Time and Space

Suddenly, I was again whirling through time and space. My view opened to new scenes; I saw the history of the world unfold on a huge panoramic screen. Life seemed like a puzzle with pieces falling into place. It was so exhilarating! I thought of how people on earth think programs on TV or in movies are exciting, but they pale when compared to our own fascinating world's history.

I had heard a lot of negative things about the world and its history, but just as in my own day, in years past much good had gone unnoticed. It probably always would until everything is known on the Other Side.

I saw that fashions and standards of beauty changed over the years. My attention focused on a scene where I saw a fairly large, portly woman who was considered a true beauty in her time. She was posing semi-nude for a painting, and I realized that everyone could someday view not only the painting, but her posing for it.

Instantly, I knew she felt proud to be posing for this painting but there would come a time when she would regret it. At this moment, however, she was proud of herself, her beauty, and her roly-poly figure. I chuckled when I thought of all the poor thin women of her day who envied her full figure. They disliked their looks and felt lacking in feminine beauty because their bodies did not match their time-period's standard of loveliness when it was fashionable to be plump.

Beauty Standards Are Passing Fads

The beauty standard in my time was almost an exact opposite. I learned that the *fat* or *thin* question was a *passing fad* that passed with time and was not important in heaven. With a stark realization, I knew that while on earth we may be teased or belittled if our size or looks do not match the current standard of beauty. However, the standards by which we are judged on earth change often and are not of lasting significance.

I knew that a healthy body at an ideal weight for each person's frame (not thin) would become fashionable. I was surprised to learn this about weight; it was such a big issue during my lifetime. I was surprised to learn that being overweight did not reap ridicule on the Other Side as it does in earth life. However, there is obvious wisdom in eating right.

Heavenly Treasures Don't Go Out of Style
"People and family are more important than things"

Glimpses of men and women were shown me who desired to be in style and in vogue with fashions that changed with the whims and fads of their time. I knew that they sacrificed important things in their lives for fancy clothes, jewelry, and other material things, to stay at the height of whatever was considered the "in thing" at the time. It seemed silly to me from my Other Side viewpoint, and I learned how important it was to keep a balance. Priorities needed to be grounded by an eternal perspective of heavenly treasures that did not wear out or go out of style.

As the years passed and styles changed, I saw that apparel which had been so important lost its appeal as the newest or latest fashion was desired instead. After people who had been caught up in fashion trends passed on to the Other Side, they became aware of the foolishness of their behavior. They were disappointed in themselves for wasting their time and resources on frivolous earthly things when they found out that *people and family were so much more important than things.*

⁓

Chapter 22

History, Journals, and Marvels to Come

ON THE OTHER SIDE, words are not required for clear understanding because all thoughts and intentions are known and understood with clarity.

Words that have been spoken, however, do not just disappear into the air; they remain and can be tuned into and understood. I believe I could have heard anything from the Beatitudes to the Gettysburg Address just as if I were there when they were first uttered. All words are still present if the time is right to tune into them. As I realized that all thoughts, words, and deeds are waiting for review on the Other Side, I wished I could call back all the words I had spoken in harshness.

New Dimensions of Understanding

Everything I saw over there was communicated to me with clear understanding. Some scenes were separate from others and some were connected, although it was as if they were all still present. Time has a different dimension in the spiritual realm. Describing it as a fourth dimension seems inadequate. If Einstein gave us four dimensions of space and time in his theories of relativity, then I would call this the fifth dimension. I have learned since my near death experience that a physicist friend of mine, who has done research in this area, calls the fifth dimension the eternity domain. Also, I have learned that he has scientific evidence that space and time are earthly limitations.

The Importance of Journals

I wanted to communicate to my posterity. I realized it would have been valuable to have left them a written account of what I had learned during earth life. But now I couldn't—I didn't have my body anymore.

In the spiritual sphere, I saw and felt the importance of writing in diaries or journals and keeping track of family history. I realized keenly that as a person grows and develops in life, it is important to leave a written account of the lessons we learn through life so that others who follow may benefit from our experiences. I understood the importance of learning from the personal experiences of others.

The difficulty and yet the importance of conveying to posterity the lessons learned during earth life was profoundly impressed upon my mind! Also, I knew that journals and family history accounts could be visible gifts of love for posterity to read. Through them people could get to know their ancestors and have an understanding of who they were and what they believed.

Family history and journals could make it possible for posterity to continue worthwhile traditions, develop their own family traditions, and have a better chance to avoid pitfalls that may have plagued other family members before them.

During earth life, I had occasionally written in journals, but I didn't keep it up. I had many excuses and believed my journals would not be interesting to anyone. However, I saw that someday some of my posterity—my children's children and their children—would be interested in reading my journals and their family history. They would want to know about me, their great-great-grandmother, who had lived before them during earth life.

Leaving a Gift in Writing—a Family History

Previously, I had thought of myself as a daughter, granddaughter, and great-granddaughter, but now I realized I would also be a great-grandmother and great-great-grandmother, and so on. I had never really thought about *posterity*, other than my grandchildren who were already born, until I had this glimpse of them. Then I knew the importance of leaving them a written account of their family history. I had an overwhelming desire to communicate to them, to let them know that I cared.

As I thought of the love and concern I had for my previously unknown future family members, they did not seem too distant or too many to know and love. Love is limitless and has no bounds.

Thinking about the importance of family journals, I knew that the tone of the messages within them needed to be positive and upbeat—not writings that might hurt or embarrass another person, or things that someone might decide to tear up and throw away. They needed to be uplifting, yet true.

It became evident how much power there is in saying good things about others and keeping a record of the highlights of life, yet not disregarding challenges or pitfalls. I realized the need of emphasizing messages such as to "keep on keeping on," to look for blessings and to record miracles. It was also important to keep the writings focused on overcoming and learning so that posterity could look back and grow from what was shared with them.

There was great value, I now knew, in writing and sharing messages of hope and encouragement—nuggets of knowledge and wisdom learned from the journey of life.

Some people have suggested writing down bad experiences, even venomous words and the worst of feelings; but for every action, even writing down feelings, there is absolutely a reaction. Forgiving, letting go, and loving unconditionally are worthwhile thoughts and actions that will be multiplied for the good of all concerned, especially when recording events and feelings in journals. *Words are powerful!*

Heavenly Stress-Reducers

My thoughts expanded with an increased awareness of many people living on earth during my lifetime and how they suffered under burdens of stress unique to our period of the world's ongoing history. I became aware of many things that could decrease stress, such as overcoming negative patterns of *reacting* to other people with anger, and following wise counsel as taught in scriptures such as "judge not that ye be not judged." I knew that the more scriptural teachings were followed, the more stress would be relieved.

I also knew that during earth life, being empathetic and less easily offended adds to peace of mind which will extend to the Other Side.

Present and Future

My view did not end with the past or present; the panorama continued into the future. I recall that it seemed humorous to me that I once thought the present was so advanced, technologically and otherwise, because it is still in the "dark ages" compared to what will be forthcoming in the future.

I was truly inspired to realize how earth knowledge and technology will continue to advance and expand. For instance, great discoveries and improvements will be made in what is considered "conventional" medical treatments. Alternate fields of healing will be more accepted and there will be faster, more accurate diagnostic techniques and treatments. Other technological advances, I learned, would dwarf what I knew during my earth life.

My feelings about so many things were changed from seeing history happen. Again, it was like seeing puzzle pieces that had been randomly scattered finally fit together.

Chapter 23

~

Eternal Beauty Secrets

ABRUPTLY, MY VIEW OF the scenes and the panorama of the history of earth ended and the spirit world was again revealed. I was surprised as I realized more about God's ever-present and observable love. Feeling His love was glorious and beautiful—a beauty that encompassed everything and everyone in my view.

It is difficult to describe the beauty of the people I saw and felt in the spiritual sphere; it was incredible. I am not talking about outer beauty, but a loveliness that came from deep within and enhanced physical features.

This inner radiance had nothing to do with age. In fact, age itself was interesting; it seemed to me that everyone I saw or of whom I was aware was at their ideal age although there were those who seemed older and those who seemed younger. I do not believe those who appeared older were actually older spirits; perhaps they looked that way for my view.

Goodness Is Beauty

In earth life, youth and beauty had seemed so connected. On the Other Side, I was surprised that two spirits who were among the most attractive were a man and a woman who looked older to me. Their faces were creased with wrinkles and I realized that each of their wrinkles was a visual testament of the lives they had led in mortality.

My understanding was opened and I became aware of the sorrows and trials this man and woman had withstood in life. Each wrinkle seemed to be a badge of valor that stood for their righteous concerns, a crisis, or an ongoing struggle they had weathered with success. Each line seemed to tell a story; every action, every thought, pain, and concern were known. They were beautiful people because of their mercy, compassion, patience, and love for others. I was awed because I had never considered wrinkles in the face as attractive, but they were to me now, as I understood what these people had gone through, and knew of their tears and pleas to God for mercy and help for others.

Then I began noticing other faces more carefully. There were some who were marred by the lines in their faces. Since every action and thought was known, I knew that many of these lines had been formed by frowning, scowling, excessive anger, and mean-spiritedness. Their faces reflected their former enjoyment of gloating, hurting, and taking advantage of others while on earth. These choices were now causing them anguish and sorrow.

The Beauty Within

What a contrast! Suddenly I understood a great truth about beauty. On earth, I believed beauty came from youth and flawless features. In the spirit world, it became obvious that beauty is created from loving, caring, charitable thinking and actions—by endurance through trials with good attitudes. It came from within and was manifested in the outer appearance.

I saw many who had been considered plain and homely on earth accepted among the most lovely, according to the way they had conducted themselves while in mortality. I saw that those who had an illusion of beauty while in mortality would be seen by eyes of new understanding on the Other Side. They would be perceived from every angle. They had a special radiance if they had conducted themselves well while in their earthly life.

All Good Deeds Are Rewarded

My concept of beauty was greatly expanded to include my view of each individual as a whole person with their inner self and their outer beauty radiating a loving countenance, or lack of it. Looks from an earthly perspective were insignificant in the afterlife.

I received the marvelous knowledge that all good thoughts and deeds are eventually rewarded and add to a person's eternal, radiating countenance.

Chapter 24

~

Caring Relationships Do Not End at Death

It was impressed upon me that heavenly, caring relationships begin on earth and do not end at death. In fact, they can be stronger and even more special on the Other Side.

I observed both men and women there and I was aware that we maintain the same gender as in life. I remained me—a woman and a mother who greatly cared about her family. I was a daughter concerned about her mother, and I knew that relationships of family and friends continue and we can be reunited with our loved ones who have passed on.

Suddenly I felt very alone. My marriage on earth had not worked out. I felt no blame or unkind feelings; in fact I had a new understanding and sorrow for our differences and problems. I was sorry for any of my wrong actions or reactions, yet we were not right for each other.

However, I knew that friendship, companionship, and the relationships between men and women can be special—more than I had ever realized before. This magnified my loneliness and my desire for another chance at earth life to find a companion so that we might enjoy the journey of life together.

My thoughts were immediately filled with the all-encompassing love from God. As I rejoiced and felt encircled in His love, I knew that the added love of the companion I desired would have been an extra joy because God's love is so great it dissolved all my feelings that I was unloved.

I experienced a sharp awareness of an increased love and caring for my family and friends. My concern wasn't only for those people with whom I now felt ties, but also for people I had hardly known, or had not previously known who were connected to me.

Happy Homecoming or Lost Blessings

I became aware of many of my ancestors including some I had heard about as a child. The knowledge came to me that if we have met the challenges in life and then died (that is if our arrival on the Other Side is not due to our own misguided actions) we are received in an attitude of homecoming. We are greeted with a great outpouring of love from those on the Other Side who have been anxiously watching and who have been eager for us to succeed on earth in our mortal school. Ancestors and posterity are concerned for our success during our earth life and exist in a sphere close to us even though we cannot see them with our mortal eyes. Our ancestors love and care for us and we love them. *We are important to each other.*

However, those who do something to cause their own death—commit suicide, or give up and regrettably will themselves to die when it's not their time as I did—may have feelings of real sadness for blessings that were lost by their own actions. Also, there may be a turning away of loved ones, posterity and ancestors whom we let down. Especially ancestors who had endured difficulties, suffered, and sacrificed for their posterity, may turn away rather than welcome someone's untimely arrival on the Other Side.

Ancestors Are Great Supporters

There were no greater supporters, I realized, than my ancestors who had paved my way with their actions and their very lives. I remember that there were many—some were dressed in angelic white robes and others in clothing that seemed appropriate for differing periods of history. I was aware that they could appear to me in different attire if it would help my understanding.

Their manner of dress was not impressed on my mind as vividly as was my discomfort in being with them; I wanted to retreat from their presence. Their exact words were not clear but I understood that they wanted to convey definite messages of love and concern. They were sad that I had given up. I knew that most of them had endured many more physical hardships than I had faced on earth and yet they did not give up. Knowing this, I felt great sorrow that I had not done better with my earth time. These feelings of regret were woven like threads through my entire experience on the Other Side.

Ancestral Cheerleaders

My ancestors cared about the decisions I made, my actions, and my happiness. Their attitudes could best be described as mental and spiritual cheerleaders. I learned that there are many people interested in each of our lives—more than I ever imagined. As I realized my importance to them, I knew how disappointed they were when I cheated myself by willing myself to die instead of making the most of my opportunities.

While I was on the Other Side, I was aware that when I was alive on earth and influenced by anger, false pride, or sin, I repelled rather than attracted special spiritual blessings. I saw that when I was tempted to give up on life, to think and act contrary to God's laws, I was vulnerable to influence by spirits who desired my failure, depression, and sadness. Those dark spirits found satisfaction when I wandered from my goals in life and forfeited peace of mind on the Other Side. I knew they were *real* and as desirous of my failure as my spiritual and ancestral cheerleaders were of my success.

Getting Rid of the Influence of Dark Spirits

The realization came to me that these darker spirits were unable to reach me when I chose positive, uplifting thoughts and activities—especially when I prayed, or read scriptures and pondered their spiritual messages! I had my freedom to choose what to think and what to do, and God was there to help me with my choices. *Dark spirits have limitations and could have only influenced my thoughts if I permitted them to.*

Knowing that thoughts create attitudes and then produce actions, I learned the importance of controlling thoughts. I recognized wrongful patterns such as envy, anger, and hurtful actions for what they had been—dangers to my lasting happiness.

Spiritual Showers

As I wondered how to combat the efforts of dark spirits, I thought about comparing a cleansing shower with reading and pondering scriptures. Scripture study was like a spiritual shower because it caused the dark spirits to disappear; they recoiled in the presence of Godly things. I could have felt spiritually clean and more receptive to inspiration by studying great eternal truths, more capable of living a Godlike life, and more able to take part in God's Grand Plan.

It was now clear that there are many truths and answers in scriptures and other Great Books of Holy Writings which could have given me a more righteous perspective and a more abundant life. The path of life for lasting peace is detailed there. For example, in the wisdom contained in the Beatitudes and in the scripture, *Inasmuch as ye do it unto the least of them, ye have done it unto me* [God].

However, I realized these books could not give guidance if they were not read! I knew that reading them, studying them prayerfully, and pondering them, would allow knowledge to enter the mind and opens the channel of inspiration and understanding for a higher way of living that causes dark spirits to flee. Now I understood how *literally true, yet understated the scriptures are.*

Stepping Stones to Wisdom

As I understood the wisdom and eternal success principles found in the scriptures and how powerful they were, all the thousands of books written to help everyone come to the same conclusions seemed irrelevant. Most of them would not be necessary if scriptures were really *studied, understood,* and *applied* in our lives. However, I also realized that the myriad of books and self-improvement courses can be stepping-stones leading to better understanding and application of the teachings of the Great Books—knowledge of eternal truths help us overcome the stumbling blocks in the journey of life.

Chapter 25

∽

Lasting Peace of Mind

IT WAS SURPRISING TO learn how much God loves and appreciates the sincere and devout of all faiths who seek to better themselves and aid humanity. The love of God abounds for all—He is no respecter of persons of one over another. Never before had I felt so connected with all people and all religions as I did when I realized the extent of His love. He has such rich rewards waiting for those who sincerely strive to follow Him.

I wondered why there were so many religions on earth, and I wondered about their greatly varying teachings, scriptures, and interpretations of them. It was shown to me that some teachings in different religions in the world are nearer to God's truths than others. Those that are closest are generally found in some form in all religions; for example, treating others as we would have them treat us. I was keenly aware that we are all at our own level of spiritual beliefs and at our own level of ability to live by religious teachings. I had a bright awareness that God is pleased with all those who strive for righteousness.

Hungering and Thirsting for Righteousness

As people fervently and sincerely seek to know the truth and to live God's laws, He is pleased, and their spiritual selves are expanded. They become capable of receiving more inspiration, knowledge, and truth; *they reap blessings.* I knew that the more people apply the knowledge and inspiration they are given, the more they can receive.

I was also shown that there were many people who were complacent and unwisely satisfied with what they believe. Yet I was aware that there were vast numbers of people sincerely striving to gain answers to life's questions and knowledge of Eternal Truths. Driven by a great hunger and thirst for righteousness, they sample the teachings of many religions of the world. Seeking to drink from a "living well," they rightly search until they find the religion that gives them guidance and inner peace.

These sincere people look for the religion they believe is right for them and that fulfills their quest for knowledge about their own true purpose for living.

Nothing Is Too Small for God's Concern

My wonderment continued as I realized how all-knowing God is. No care or problem is too small for Him to know everything about it.

I realized that God offers a peace beyond comprehension or description, an eternal peace of mind! I had never even imagined that God was so all-knowing. As my understanding was opened, I knew He is fully aware of everyone's problems, temptations, and sorrows. He is aware of sincerity, righteous sacrifices, and the intent of each heart as His children strive to live by His commandments.

My being was filled with love and appreciation for the sincere believers of all the world's religions. I understood that God's Holy Words offer a lasting peace beyond worldly description for all. The greatest and most lasting peace of mind for earth life and the Other Side is offered to all humanity by God.

Chapter 26

⁓

Prayer, Promptings, and Whisperings of the Spirit

NEXT, I SAW AND became aware of many aspects of prayer and how important it is to pray. Learning that prayer truly is a conversation with God, I realized that He wanted to hear from me and to communicate with me. I then knew the importance of expressing gratitude and appreciation for all my blessings—from small things to great miracles.

Connecting to Heavenly Power

Feeling remorse that I had taken for granted many special blessings, I now saw my life in its proper perspective. I knew that electricity was powerful and capable of mighty accomplishments when something is connected to it. But I saw that being connected to heavenly power in prayer is an infinitely greater power that draws from a "heavenly treasury." I knew that miracles are possible and happen much more frequently than acknowledged on earth.

During my earth life, I had not adequately realized this amazing source of power. Many times I prayed from habit or because I needed something in particular. But at this point, I saw prayer, silent and spoken, as a two-way communication with someone I loved and respected, who loved me and had the power to bless me for my good. In my life review, I saw that many of my prayers had been granted, and I felt remorse that I had not recognized and expressed appreciation for my blessings.

Knowledge was given to me about "No" answers to prayers and how they had been for my benefit. Also, I more fully realized the great importance of doing what I could with what I had and appreciating it, rather than concentrating on and lamenting over what I did not have.

My mind was quickened with the knowledge that there were answers to prayers and blessings I had received where I had falsely given the credit to "coincidence," instead of giving thanks to God in all things.

Visualizing a Personal God

Knowledge was given to me about the importance of praying regularly and thinking of God as a person. There were times when I used to pray and my mind would wander because I did not have a clear understanding and mental picture of God. I was thrilled to know that He is an actual Being who has feelings and that He loves me. This was not just some cloud I was speaking to when I knelt in prayer. I discovered He is much more knowledgeable, understanding, and loving than any other person I could ever imagine knowing.

Receiving Answers to Prayers

My awareness was opened to some of the many things involved in receiving answers to prayers, such as the sincerity of mind and heart and the *readiness* of the person to receive the requested help asked for. Sometimes an answer to a prayer to have a burden removed comes in the form of strength to carry it rather than a miracle to take the burden or problem away.

Also, I saw the definite connection between the likelihood of receiving mercy and help requested to the mercy and help the person praying has given others. Knowledge was given me that God usually uses willing people to answer others' prayers. I became aware that our prayers are more apt to be answered when we ask and respond positively to the questions *"Whose burden could I lighten today as I ask God to help ease mine? Who is waiting to hear from me?* **With wisdom**, *whose pain could I ease with loving words or deeds so I could then ask with a clear conscience for my prayer to be answered?"*

God is keenly aware of everyone's prayers. It is unproductive to ask Him to answer our prayers when we deliberately ignore the needs of those we ought to be mindful of—especially elderly parents and grandparents who wait to hear or need help from children and loved ones.

Scenes came to my mind of people on earth who were preoccupied with their babies and other children to the extent that they neglected aging parents and grandparents who had expended their time, strength, and means caring for them when they were young.

As the years rolled by, some of the elderly parents in the scenes I viewed became so weak that they were no longer able to care for themselves. They needed attention from their children and grandchildren. Because they felt lost and forgotten, they gave up and simply waited to die. What a difference a visit, a phone call, or a card would have made to them. They waited day after day with no contact from even their closest loved ones—those on whom they had spent their own time and resources.

Watching and hearing older parents and grandparents praying and asking God to ease their burdens and loneliness made me feel great sadness for all concerned. I was aware that many promptings to their children to make those requested calls or visits were sadly unheeded. Yet, the children and grandchildren were asking God to answer their own prayers while they were oblivious to those whose prayers *they* could so easily answer.

Take Time to Listen to the Whisperings of the Spirit

I learned that while praying to God, expressing gratitude, and asking for blessings, it is also very important to pause and take time to listen to *promptings* that may come as *whisperings* from the Holy Spirit. Promptings may be blocked by becoming too caught up in "asking." Only when we take time to *listen* can we receive the inspiration, promptings, and guidance that brings peace beyond measure.

Continually asking for blessings, I realized, without giving sincere thanks, is like a child asking a parent for more and more without taking time to give thanks and appreciation for what has already been received. God wants to receive thanks as do earthly parents.

I Longed to Return to My Body

Vividly aware of how my decisions and actions could so personally affect the lives of others and myself, I longed for the chance to come back and make right what I could; to progress and grow through life and not run from it. I wanted to come back and change whatever ill effects my death would cause others, and to use my earth time more effectively.

Although I had not actually committed suicide, I had completely surrendered my life, willing myself to die, and God had granted my desire. Now, in this sphere, the implications of my choices were clear. Starkly apparent were things that I wanted to do on earth that I had not done and could have done. Thoughts of my family came again to my mind and I wanted to tell them what I had learned about the Other Side.

Heavenly Answers Discovered

Also, I wanted to tell others who were looking for hope about the heavenly answers to problems on earth that I had discovered. I wanted to shout the real value of life on earth and the foolishness of trying to cut life short to escape problems and physical discomforts.

When I saw things in the proper perspective, I wanted to live even in an aching, mortal body. Every part of my mind, heart, and spirit begged to have another chance to go back to the earthly sphere. Feelings of "if only" were tormenting me.

I was struck with the knowledge that in earth life, it was not how physically impaired one is that matters or what physical abilities were gone; rather, it was how one used what was left. I was desperately willing to be once again shackled with my physical limitations.

In the spiritual sphere, I was free from physical pain for the first time in many long years, yet the emotional anguish I was feeling was many times worse than the physical pain I'd had when I was alive. I wanted to escape this spiritual misery even more than I had wanted to escape my physical pain.

Unhappily, I felt that asking to return was useless. I had lived my life. I had had the chance to live or die and had chosen to die. I had prayed for death and here it was. It seemed futile to request another chance, yet I couldn't stop myself. The more I thought about the opportunities I had let slip past me, the more I wanted to be allowed to return.

~

Chapter 27

Drawn Back into My Earthly Body

The Truth about a Tooth

Suddenly a huge tooth appeared before me as if it were hanging in the air. It was enlarged many times, giving me views of its surfaces. It was my gold-crowned tooth and I knew which one. In fact, I knew most everything about it—its history throughout my life, its growth, and its period of great usefulness. The tooth had been crowned at least fifteen years earlier.

During all those years I had not given that tooth any thought because it had not given me any pain. I had a thorough dental checkup not long before this experience, and all my teeth checked out fine. But as information about this particular tooth was given me, I knew that it was a serious problem and was an important part of the answer to recovering my physical health.

A Gift of Knowledge

Before this experience, I did not know that such a simple thing as a tooth could cause or contribute to so much damage to health. This vivid and complete gift of knowledge about my tooth played a vital part in the possibility that I could live again in my physical body, although I did not know why at that instant.

Mortally Alive Again

Just as suddenly as it had appeared, the tooth vanished and I was quickly drawn back into my body. Still leaning forward toward the inside of the tub, I stared at the bottom of the bathtub for a while, realizing that miraculously I was back on earth. I began trying to push myself up from the edge of the tub. Slowly, I made my body move. My fingers moved; I gradually moved my hands and I touched my face. I was solid, mortally alive again!

Turning my head, I noted with amazement that I could only see what was in my normal field of vision. The "everywhere at once" vision I'd had in the spirit world was gone.

A Return to Earth Life

Immediately, I was aware of physical pain; I ached throughout my whole body. There were sharp pains in my arms, legs, hands, and feet, and I had very little strength. My weakness was so profound that it made gravity seem powerful and oppressive. But I didn't care. I had no desire to exchange my situation of pain and sickness for that light, floaty, pain-free existence. I was being given another chance at life!

The anguish was gone; my agony of spirit was over. Kneeling shakily and leaning on the tub, I felt the glorious thrill of once again being alive and on the earth. My pleas to return to earth life had been granted. Gratitude welled up inside of me. Joy and relief overwhelmed me. I was overjoyed to be where I was; even grateful to feel exhausted, to feel my body's pain, and to feel ill.

I tried to get back into bed and found that I couldn't walk; even crawling was difficult. The effort was exhausting because I was so weak and my movements were slow. But all the way I kept thinking, "I can move my body. I am alive!"

Gratitude beyond Expression

Uncertain as to how long I had been on the Other Side, I was overjoyed to have returned. The gratitude I felt was beyond my ability to express. Thinking of how, only a short time before, I was wishing for release from my earthly existence, now I was ecstatic to have returned to life in any physical condition.

Even though I was ill, I now knew that being alive was a great blessing. I was determined to stop putting limitations on my body by thinking negative thoughts about my health. My body was precious and priceless no matter what it looked like or how ill it was.

No Clocks Needed on the Other Side

Managing to get back into bed, earth life seemed to be the *foreign* sphere where time and clocks were odd. The Other Side was the natural sphere where no clocks were needed. There I experienced a dimension of time where everything was *now*—where a person's intent of the heart and words were not misinterpreted, and where all truth was known. That was the *real* sphere.

Back for How Long?

Knowing the significance of returning to earth life, though, and being thrilled that I could speak again, I said aloud, "I am back, I am really back." Tears of joy spilled down my cheeks. Then concerns struck me.

I'm back, but for how long?

How long will I be given to do the things I want to do in earth life?

How long will I have to put into practice the perspectives that I gained?

No answer came to me. Knowing that I had no guarantees, no idea of the length of time I was being given, I knew I had to make every moment count. Being anxious to get busy living, I wanted to stand up and start right then. My weakness, though, was such that I could only lie there and contemplate how much I had learned, and how much I wanted to do.

When I felt somewhat stronger, I made my way into the family room where Crystal's foolish video game—my gift to her—was located. She had not been at my home for a couple of days. Slowly, I unhooked the game from the back of the TV set, gathered up the cords and controllers, and hid them away. Then I returned to bed.

The experience I had and the scenes I had viewed which contained symbolic, life-changing messages for me seemed miraculous. Wanting to tell anyone who would listen, I soon told those I trusted the most. My experience was sufficiently personal, though, that I was careful with whom I shared it.

Scenes from the Spiritual Realm

Scenes of Crystal's posterity were still so vivid in my mind that I felt I could almost step back into that sphere where I had seen them and again be a part of that spiritual realm. Never again did I want to be responsible for this game's possible burdens of guilt.

The next time Crystal came, she was upset that the game was gone, but being an easygoing child, she soon adjusted and began doing other worthwhile things. She took more interest in her schoolwork and even talked of wanting to go to college when old enough.

Although it wasn't easy giving up my electronic baby-sitter, it was well worth it as I received peace of mind seeing Crystal grow mentally and spiritually by finding better ways of using her time.

Note: As Crystal matured, she continued using her time in productive ways and went on to college. She married, has four children and a grandson, who is my great-great-grandson. Several of the posterity I viewed on the Other Side have since been born on earth. I'm grateful that

I have lived to see and know on earth so many of my additional posterity. Hopefully they will learn what they need to from their time on earth. I certainly pray they do.

Between Two Spheres

Throughout the next two weeks, I felt the odd sensation that at anytime, night or day, I could step back into that other sphere, the spirit world. The knowledge I had gained was still fresh in my mind. I could call up the images I had seen at will and re-experience my visit there. Memories of the larger picture of life and life after death impressed upon my mind that earth life is very temporary.

Although I wanted to be alive with all my heart, I did not want to lose my enlightenment, my knowledge, and the new awareness I had gained. I hoped this bright awareness and access to the Other Side would last the rest of my life, but gradually I felt the spirit world begin to slip away. With my new knowledge, I understood that I could not continue to live on earth unless I was able to experience life's trials and temptations in a natural way, and little by little I re-entered mortality and felt a part of earth life once more.

PART FOUR

My Life

after

I Returned

to Earth

Chapter 28

~

The Dentist—My Friend

AMONG MY MOST VIVID memories of the Other Side was the importance of getting that tooth removed. Gathering my strength, I made an appointment with my dentist, and asked my mom to take me to see him. I told him of the particular gold-crowned tooth in my mouth that needed to be pulled. He looked at the one in question and shook his head.

"Does it hurt?" he asked.

"No."

"It looks and seems okay," he said positively.

"It may look okay, but it has to come out," I emphatically replied.

He tried to reassure me that I was worrying needlessly. He took an X-ray to appease me. As he showed it to me, he smiled and said, "Joyce, just as I thought, there is nothing wrong with this tooth." He showed me the X-ray, carefully explaining why the tooth was sound.

However, its appearance on the X-ray did not impress me; I absolutely *knew* that the tooth had to be extracted. In my mind, I again saw the tooth—gold crowned, suspended, rotating in front of me. Something was wrong with that tooth and I knew it had to come out. To convince my dentist, I decided to share parts of my experience with him.

He listened carefully and politely, then shook his head slowly, "You know, Joyce, I'm limited to the practice of Western medicine. Nothing I've studied has prepared me professionally to believe I need to take out that tooth. This experience you had just isn't enough for me."

My dentist was a respected professional and he had a way of making his patients feel he was their friend; he treated us with sincerity and concern. He and I had a good rapport, and he could see I was determined to have this particular tooth extracted.

He sighed, paused, and then continued, "Still, if you insist, you'll need to sign a form releasing me from liability for pulling a tooth just because you believe it should come out."

I readily agreed. He said he would make the necessary arrangements, including the liability-release form, and suggested a later date for its removal. He had injured his hand and could not extract my tooth just then. Disappointed because I was determined to have the tooth taken out immediately, I said, "I really want to get it out right away."

Clearly, he did not know what to make of my persistence. He shook his head again and then patiently told me, "If you feel it can't wait, the best I can do is refer you to a colleague."

Reluctantly he gave me the name of an oral surgeon. His receptionist called the oral surgeon's office and arranged an immediate appointment. My dentist let me take the X-ray of my tooth to the appointment so an additional one would not be required.

My Tooth, the Villain

I explained to the oral surgeon that I wanted to keep the tooth after its removal. He anesthetized my mouth, extracted the tooth, and showed it to me. As we stared at it;

he shook his head in dismay.

As we examined the tooth, I was stunned. The roots were a peculiar darkened color, and even to my untrained eye it was obvious they had deteriorated. They were oddly shaped and looked as if they had melted. The oral surgeon said very little as he examined the tooth while showing it to me. He placed it in a container for me and I left.

Electrical Needles and Pins

As I was leaving his office and for an hour or two afterwards, I felt strange sensations—as though thousands of electrical needles and pins were embedded in the skin all over my body and were working their way out to the surface through all of my pores. It was very uncomfortable. Within twenty-four hours, the mysterious bleeding down the back of my throat stopped as though a tap had been turned off. I was extremely grateful.

A few days after the extraction, I took the tooth back to my regular dentist on a follow-up visit and he examined it closely. He asked if he could cut it in half to observe the interior. I agreed. Silver amalgam filling could be seen beneath the gold. (Until my experience on the Other Side, I didn't know about the severe health problems that could be caused by teeth *or* that silver-mercury amalgam or gold and silver in the same tooth could cause health problems.)

He gave the tooth back to me cut into two pieces. He agreed it was a good thing it was out.

A Miraculous Recovery

Within a few days, I went back to see the ear, nose, and throat specialist and took the gold-crowned tooth to show him. He held up half of it at a time with a pair of tweezers and examined it closely. He was usually a quiet man of few words who went in and out of the examination room briskly. Not this time. He looked from the roots of the tooth, to me, then back to the roots of the tooth. He exclaimed emphatically, "Joyce, I never would have gotten you well with that in your mouth."

He told me the roots apparently had been embedded in the sinuses and had been "dissolved" by the infection. The infected tooth was the cause of the internal bleeding from my sinuses and had become too much for my system to overcome.

A Gift from God

My delight at receiving that gift from God was soon joined by other blessings. Within two or three weeks the intense pain from my arthritis was almost completely gone. I began recovering miraculously in many ways and my rheumatoid arthritis went into remission.

≈   ≈   ≈

Joyce—back from the afterlife and grateful to be alive

Chapter 29

⁓

The Test That Hurt

SHORTLY AFTER MY OTHER Side experience, I enthusiasti-
cally told several people close to me about it. However, I
carefully pondered the entire occurrence and had mixed
feelings about sharing it—this subject wasn't openly discussed at that time. Also, this experience was sacred and
personal to me.

I was extremely excited about returning to earth's mortal sphere. In some ways, I wanted to tell everyone what I
had learned: *Heavenly answers to earthly challenges are available for all and so is the knowledge that permits us to be certain
of enjoying the Other Side when we get there.*

Shortly after coming back, I remember wishing I
could grab a megaphone and shout my message from the
tallest building. When another individual's need to hear
about my experience on the Other Side became apparent, I shared it with assurance. At that time, I felt I was
one of the most confident people on earth. I knew who
I was: *a child of God!* For quite awhile after my experience, I didn't think I'd ever fear being in the presence of
other people again.

Gradually though, as time passed, my self-confidence

in speaking about my experience began to dim. As I settled back into earth life, my experience and the lessons I had learned began to slip to the back of my mind rather than being the focus of my attention daily.

A "Test" of My Ability to Forgive

During the first few weeks after my return I was grateful for each problem awaiting me, because I knew of the benefits I could receive when I overcame them. By understanding problems in their proper eternal perspective, I realized that each difficult experience, well lived with sincere intentions, was like a jewel on a crown. Its message would sparkle with rewards for having triumphed and passed through a refiner's fire. I knew that progressing through life would be enormously easier if I remembered to evaluate events from the eternal perspective.

The attitude I took in any given situation was my choice! With my new eternal outlook at that time, I was able to see life's experiences in a different way. Trials were blessings, and I wanted to make it through them with the right attitude.

Realizing the rewards to be received by forgiving others, I wanted to forgive everyone for everything. By knowing that offenses to me could be opportunities to forgive others, I later wondered if I might have "issued an unfortunate invitation" for problems after my return to earth life because of what happened concerning a valuable business contract.

Suspicions arose that my agents were working behind the scenes to cut me out of my twenty-year contract which provided environmental services to a governmental entity. Finally, after tremendous efforts by all of my business-team members, our suspicions were confirmed. Evidence surfaced between 1984 and 1986 that my agents, instead of working in my behalf as required by my contract, had attempted to take it for themselves.

Unknown to me, my agents had created a new company and my associates and I were excluded from critical and required meetings. Contrary to our contractual agreements, my contract was assigned to this new unknown company and listed as their own asset in legal documents. After they breached my contract, it was finally lost for both of us.

However, a substantial amount of money was owed me for my share of the project's earlier revenues. But in 1986 on the day I was to receive the check from my agents, I was told I would need an attorney to get it. I was devastated. Reluctantly, I pursued legal action.

The Wondrous Results of Sleep Teaching

After the valuable contract was breached and its benefits lost for all concerned, including the project's employees, I needed help to get hold of my thinking. I called upon all my past experiences and resources to design, create, and develop a more powerful Sleep Teaching course than any I had used before. It had positive suggestions to help me sleep and to help me handle the stress and to think and feel better.

Listening to those positive suggestions helped keep my thoughts and actions more in tune with the principles I had learned on the Other Side for a higher way of living. I used them continuously. Gradually I made it hour by hour and day by day. The special Sleep Teaching courses with Super-Subliminals™ and with Whisper Learning™ worked wonders.

Because the courses were unique and produced results, I had requests from people who wanted to purchase them and offers from others who wanted to market them. But I was trapped in a legal web and could not fill the requests at that time. The lost revenues for the unfilled orders was considerable.

Mortal Guardian Angels

Due to the significance of the legal complexities regarding my breached contract, it was necessary that I retain several attorneys to represent me. After almost four years of unproductive litigation, miraculously, I was blessed to acquire Roger Magnuson as my lead attorney. He is a fine person, and as an attorney he is exceptional and highly respected both nationally and internationally. He is known as an expert on the subject and is the author of the book, *White Collar Crime*. He aptly uncovered the truth and diligently fought for me. I will always have a special place in my heart for him.

An additional member of my team of attorneys who was a great help to me was James Langdon. He compassionately added his strength in guiding me through this legal storm. In the background expertly overseeing and coordinating things was Leon Halgren. Over the years, Leon has been like a guardian angel when I've needed his legal help.

Also, he wrote extremely important and timely letters with requests for documentation from this new company with which we were dealing. (They were some of the same people but had a different corporate name.) Leon's letters became very significant. He compared this new corporate entity to a "camel that had somehow gotten its nose in the tent and then wanted to take over the whole tent."

An extremely knowledgeable, capable, and dedicated business-team member, Bob Frome, has been like another guardian angel for several years. He was one of the first to recognize questionable conduct by my agents.

For so many years, Bob and Leon have been my respected attorneys, friends, and associates. There were several others who could have helped make the original project an outstanding success, and they each also had an important role in trying to rescue me from what I felt was a legal nightmare. I know they were sent in answer to my prayers although my prayers were not answered as I desired or expected.

Attorneys Everywhere

The corporation I was up against had numerous attorneys and seemed to have almost unlimited time and funds for a legal battle. The intrigue could fill a book of its own. Attorneys were everywhere, on both sides of this issue, with corresponding legal expenses. I remembered that directly after my return from the Other Side, I had wanted an opportunity to forgive and it came abundantly. For a time, my tears flowed with thoughts of "could-have-beens" and "should-have-beens" that my original contract would have produced for all concerned had it been honored. According to expert witnesses' figures as well as our own, I had lost a fortune.

With exceptional attorneys, witnesses, and evidence that seemed overwhelmingly in my favor (including written documents and statements from the company's own officers), I believe I would have won if I had had the needed strength and funds to keep fighting in the court system for the additional years that may have been required. However, I had not known what could happen by being tied up in the "justice" system, and over six years of my life had already been consumed in this legal battle. Time was on the company's side to drag it out even longer.

Earth Time Is Too Precious to Hold Grudges

Gratefully though, through Roger's skilled efforts, facts that were previously unknown to me were discovered about what had actually been taking place concerning my breached contract and stalled litigation. Facts were uncovered about important meetings that were held, monies that were paid, and agreements that had been made without my knowledge with adverse effects for my business interests. I do not believe this information would have been otherwise revealed.

Thereafter, hints began to surface that a settlement offer for several million dollars was going to be coming to me. Subsequently, though, everything seemed to stop; we heard nothing from those involved or from the court for some time. Then there was a devastating surprise ruling from the court which all of my attorneys saw as unfair and not consistent with the evidence that had been presented. It could have required months or even years of extended litigation to overcome.

The stress I had experienced dealing with this company and its spinoffs was almost unbearable. I had come to a point of depletion physically, financially, and emotionally. My Muscular Dystrophy (and more) was flaring up; I was weak and on oxygen and having difficulty breathing. I realized that I had to close those painful chapters of my life, take my losses, forgive, forget, *let go*, and withdraw from the legal battle. I knew it would cost my life to continue this fight any longer.

Then another surprise, but this time a pleasant one—an *unrequired* settlement offer was made which would almost take care of the high legal expenses I had accumulated over six years. With adjustments from my attorneys on their fees and expenses, the settlement covered their costs of this legal battle. My prayers had not been answered as I had hoped, but I knew what truly mattered was to go on with my life the best I could.

Drawing on the knowledge I gained when I was on the Other Side, I was extremely grateful to get through that very difficult period of time without being embittered. My prayers were answered with a peaceful feeling and with the assurance of rewards awaiting me on the Other Side instead of "justice" or "victory" or material blessings here. As I continued to pray, my sorrow was swallowed up in the God-given inner peace that is available to all. I knew within my heart that I had passed a *big test* because I did not have any bad feelings toward those who had hurt me with their callous actions.

At that time, I saw things in the eternal perspective, and I felt sorrow for how much they were hurting themselves and their posterity (by their bad example) when they face the consequences of their actions on the Other Side. I knew that God does not answer prayers by taking away others' free agency, and I couldn't blame God for the wrong choices others had made.

Because I knew I was exchanging my short allotment of time on earth for whatever I did that day, I was striving to look more carefully at my priorities. Time on earth is too short to remain angry or hold grudges against anyone; it is precious and limited when compared to the forever of eternity.

Earth Time Is Precious

Directly after my experience on the Other Side, with my new knowledge of the value of time, I thought that I would never again watch television or sit for hours in a movie theater. I did not want to waste one precious moment of my life. Now, however, I work at keeping a balance between worthwhile goals and needed leisure time; I do watch some television, but I am careful of quantity, content, and quality.

Learning that the type and quality of music I listen to and TV and movies I watch is worth carefully monitoring, I want the benefits of surrounding myself with inspirational and educational things rather than detrimental, destructive words or scenes.

Thoughts Are Powerful

Each hour of the day, I know that I make choices which include deliberately taking control of my thinking or allowing other forces to sway, dictate, or manipulate my thoughts and attitudes. I know that attitudes and desires are formed as a direct result of thoughts held daily in my mind, which then determine what I will accomplish during my life on earth.

Thoughts are powerful and too valuable to waste!

~

Chapter 30

Finding Hidden Benefits Reaps Rewards

Music in the Lunchroom

A FEW YEARS AGO, I became aware of a business owned by a husband and wife team. They badly needed financial backing; they were on the brink of folding a business I believed had great potential. At a meeting one evening, they were discussing the way the business would be set up after they moved to a new location. The wife was bubbling with ideas; she wanted the employees to have half a day off each week to play golf. She also wanted them to have a lunchroom where classical music would play continually and elevate them to new levels of productivity.

Her husband wanted to have western music played in the lunchroom, and he emphatically made his viewpoint known. The debate was on. Voices began to rise. The couple was getting very angry over the type of music to be played in the lunchroom of a building that hadn't even been rented yet. The lunchroom never did materialize, nor did a system on which to play any music.

A Better Perspective

Now, whenever I find myself beginning to fuss over differing points of view, I pause, take a deep breath and think, "Is this argument about music in the lunchroom?" Sometimes I laugh until tears roll down my cheeks as I stand back and see things from a better perspective.

It's amazing that people often get so involved in arguments that they could actually, physically hurt each other over something similar to "music in the lunchroom." This experience reinforced the lessons I learned on the Other Side about the futility of arguing. I find it much easier now to let others express their opinions without contradicting them. It's not up to me to challenge others' opinions and try to get them to see things my way. And I feel free from the need to defend my position—it's easier to compassionately listen and *"let it go"* if we disagree.

Do I Want Sympathy or Results?

It was clear that I had wasted a lot of time before my experience on the Other Side thinking, "Why me? Why did this happen to me?" Thoughts of "Why me, or Why now?" solve nothing and can lead to depression. Additionally, they waste valuable time and stop possible solutions that could have come to mind. It would be as if my coat caught on fire and I yelled "Why me?" as I wrung my hands while it burned rather than dousing the flames while they were still small. If I act, rather than ask "why me?" I can put out the "fire" and be grateful it wasn't worse. Then I can practice "fire prevention" in the future. Handling problems in this manner helps me find solutions rather than waste time uselessly seeking answers that will not be revealed until I view things from the Other Side's perspective.

Deadly Notions or Heavenly Rewards

On the Other Side, I became aware that there are many ways to handle problems in life. Running from them, though, and using drugs or drinking alcohol only makes them worse. Drugs and alcohol affect the chemicals in the brain and ultimately add to feeling depressed and over-whelmed—and can seriously damage health. They impair judgment and the ability to make decisions; problems of those who use them increase and compound.

Drugs, alcohol, and negative thoughts can insidiously steal life because, under their influence, people are more apt to act impulsively on the false and deadly notion that suicide is a glamorous, or acceptable way of escaping unwanted challenges—I was clearly shown that *it is not!*

Earth Time Is to Gather Good Deeds and Develop Good Character Traits

Life presents problems—working on them rather than hiding from them helps us find solutions. *Ignoring problems or blaming others does not solve them; facing them head on, praying for strength and guidance to solve them and the wisdom to find their hidden benefits, reaps great rewards.*

Others' Near-Death Experiences

On the Other Side I had questioned, "What about those who died, found a beautiful, peaceful place, and came back to earth life again? Will they find that peace next time?" The answer was given me that it depends upon the intent of their hearts and their actions as it does for all of us. My understanding was reinforced with the knowledge that *we are required to endure whatever happens to us to the end of our lives.*

However, as well as I know this, there are times when I find certain unwanted, familiar feelings starting to return, and I have to replace them with thoughts I know will help to create the actions and results I really want. Knowing that if I let my mind dwell on upsetting, unhappy thoughts, I will again attract "bad-habit thinking," I stop those thoughts by remembering what I experienced on the Other Side. The principles I learned there help me make it through difficult situations.

Helping Others Helps Me

When I am feeling stressed or not feeling as mentally "up" as I would like, I usually call someone who I know needs help. I know it does *not* help to call someone to complain about life or to criticize. A technique I have found that works wonders is to call someone with cheerful, good news or to help someone else have an "up" day. Helping someone else, usually helps me.

Also, as I share my experience with others in a way that helps them, it helps me to relive it and remember what I learned from it. Remembering the significance and reality of what I experienced continues to help me here.

For several years, my cousin Gloria, my mother, and several others, have urged me to publish my experiences, but I hesitated. Then I began receiving letters and calls from people telling me of the positive differences my story had made in the lives of those with whom I had shared; they wanted their own loved ones to know about it, too.

Ultimately, I gathered my courage and decided it was time to speak up more actively. Sometimes I speak on a one-to-one basis and other times with groups, as I feel prompted. Several times on an airplane the feeling has come to me that I must tell the person next to me a portion of my story.

When I get such feelings, they grow until I feel *compelled* to speak up. Then I begin a casual conversation and generally, with the other person's first few words, I learn why I felt impressed to speak to them. As I mentioned before, in many of life's situations, God uses people (whenever they are willing) to answer the prayers of others.

When Others Need Help

Since returning from the Other Side, there have been times that miraculous episodes have occurred when I told my story to strangers. Some needed a push to go to the dentist, others were suffering from an ailment I accurately pinpointed which they were then able to overcome by seeking proper help.

Sometimes the person was feeling depressed or suicidal, and later I learned that they made changes in their lives and were doing better. I was glad our paths crossed when they did and I was able to help.

A Gift of Empathy

Upon returning to earth life, with the new, expanded knowledge I had gained, I felt more empathetic toward others. I treasure this empathy as a gift. When I look at others' faces and countenances now, whether I am speaking to an audience, seeing someone in a restaurant, sitting next to a stranger on an airplane or almost anywhere, I seem intuitively to discern the pain and joy that the people around me have experienced in their lives.

Sensing their inner beauty, struggles, and sincerity or lack thereof, I begin to *feel* much about them. When I look into people's eyes and see their expressions, I understand them better and become aware of many of their needs, wants, fears, pains, and struggles.

Phases of History

I know we are progressing from one phase of history to another, from the past, through the present and into the future. I am extremely grateful that I was allowed to come back to earth and see some of these futuristic, remarkable things unfold. Having a better perspective helps me to understand more of what is taking place. It is fascinating to know that revolutionary technologies and marvelous inventions are coming, such as improved, new medical advances for maintaining health, outwitting disease, and *faster*, more *accurate* diagnostic techniques.

Some have already come about. It has been a marvelous experience to watch some of the things unfold that spark memories of being on the Other Side. Medical science has done almost unbelievable things, but there is yet much more to come, such as wondrous alternative-medical cures, and other natural remedies and healing discoveries for the body.

The body is a truly miraculous gift of the Creator.

Prayer and Surroundings

Prayer is a special time. After my experience on the Other Side, as I now pray, I mentally picture God in my mind as a real, loving, personable, all-wise, all-powerful, and *all-knowing* God who wants me to be grateful for what I have.

As I kneel to pray in the morning, I feel it is helpful for me to take a few moments and call to mind those whom the Lord would have me be mindful of that day. By being more aware of others' needs, I feel more in tune with God. When I am more in harmony with His desired outcome of my day, I know I am more apt to have my prayers answered favorably and to receive His peace.

Also, I prefer to get in a reverent physical and spiritual setting when I can. I do not delay my prayers, though, just because I am not in the right place or I don't look right. He listens and can hear, no matter how or where someone prays to Him. His love is extended to all, regardless of situation and apparel. Prayers are answered according to His own timetable.

When I prepare myself before praying, I feel more respectful. God is as real as any other being—certainly more special than anyone I might meet in earth life. Just as I comb my hair and straighten my appearance before opening the door to a friend or stranger, I want to do so before opening a dialogue with the most important being in my life. Prayer time can be anytime, anywhere, but I like to keep in mind with whom I am conversing, and make it special whenever I can.

My new attitude has to do with the reverence and respect I feel for Him since I have come to know Him better. Remembering the scripture that tells of Moses approaching the burning bush, the voice told him to remove his shoes, for the ground on which he stood was holy. For me now, I remind myself that prayer time is holy time, and I want to be even more respectful than I would talking with any other person.

Usually, I want to tell Him how much I sincerely appreciate what I have been given, the blessings I've received, and prayers that have been answered. It is important to thank Him for the gifts He has given before I ask for more.

It is not necessary to use eloquent speech when I pray, because I know God is understanding and knows the intent of my heart. It is important to pray in the manner I feel is comfortable and appropriate. When I was on the Other Side, I learned that He wants to hear from me—and from all of us. When I think of prayer as a two-way communication, it becomes easier to pray.

Whisperings of the Spirit

There are moments when the veil seems to draw back and memories from the Other Side return. These experiences are similar to walking into a room filled with dear and familiar people and experiences. Wondering how I could have ever forgotten some of them, I realize I didn't really forget. They are still there, but the pressures of day-to-day living pushed them to the back of my memory.

It is enjoyable when someone says something that refreshes my memory of scenes and feelings from the Other Side, and I remember how wondrously whole the purpose and plan of life really is. The combined feelings of love, connections to people, nature, knowledge about forgiveness and the desire to forgive others quickly well up within me. I re-experience some of the glorious feelings about life I felt then and deep gratitude for my mortal existence.

My love for others expanded when I learned the Great Eternal Truth that each person is a unique individual with definite, differing personalities; that we always will be known by and unconditionally loved by God. Through whisperings of the Spirit, we can all know that we have always been uniquely us even before we were born. We didn't just begin with life on earth. We can also know that our identity continues after earth life—we don't stop being us at death.

Reaping Miraculous Results

From my experience on the Other Side, I learned many things. One conclusion I reached is that life is similar to a treasure chest filled with vast treasures, for here and for heaven, but it has a big lock on it. Holding grudges, using harsh words, running from life and oneself by using drugs or alcohol and avoiding problems only makes the lock stronger.

There are "Grand Keys" to opening the lock that I learned. They are: *striving to be slow to anger, being quick to forgive, and seeking heavenly help by communicating with God through sincere prayer.*

In addition, I know that problems can be solved by believing in miracles, expecting miracles, and helping to create miraculous results for someone else. All such miracles reap eternal rewards.

Chapter 31

~

Life—Worth Living and Celebrating

WHEN MY PERSPECTIVE IS CLEAR, I gladly accept life's challenges and the size of my body. Whether I am slender or not is no longer a big issue for me. Before my near-death experience, I had been anorexic and bulimic. I had mistakenly thought that being "thin" was critically important to being happy.

However, on the Other Side, it was revealed to me and I was given knowledge and truth about the importance of having good health and that the popular desire to be thin is only a fad of present-day fashion.

Also, on the Other Side, I learned that anorexia, bulimia, or eating "junk food" can cause pain, stress, and extreme anxiety. It can kill us. How we treat our bodies can greatly determine the quality and length of our lives. The choices we make, the kinds and amounts of foods and water we eat and drink daily are definitely linked to how we think and feel.

I also learned that we need proper nourishment for body, mind, and spirit—they are absolutely intertwined. I was shown that our choices have earthly and spiritual consequences, which build or deplete our energy. *Our bodies are gifts from God, and must last us a lifetime.*

Learning more about the natural health field has been fascinating, and implementing the knowledge is a day-to-day challenge. When I nourish my mind, body, and spirit, and depend on God's timing, I have discovered profound whisperings of the Spirit and reaped *miracles*.

As I write this, I am reminded of a message I put on a wall plaque. It is from the poem "Salutation to the Dawn," author unknown. I adapted and added to this saying, and sometimes I give it out at speaking engagements:

Yesterday is already a dream, tomorrow is only a vision;
but today, WELL LIVED, makes every yesterday a dream of happiness,
and tomorrow a vision of hope.
Celebrate Life. This Is Not a Dress Rehearsal!

The Need for Help Rather than Advice

Before my near-death experience in 1983, I had tried many different things through the years to help myself, but feelings of depression and thoughts of suicide continued to creep into my mind. Their luring appeal was based on false notions of escaping from life's problems and gaining unearned peace.

Friends and family offered advice such as, "Get hold of yourself," and phrases like, "Pull yourself together! How can you be blue when you have so many blessings?" and "Snap out of it!" When I was depressed to the point of considering suicide and I would hear, "Think of your family," it only made me feel more suicidal because I wrongly felt they were selfish to ask me to live when I wanted to die.

I would caution those approached by people voicing thoughts of suicide. Statements that may seem like good advice are usually not well received by someone feeling downhearted and overwhelmed. "Get hold of yourself" type of comments do not help but add to their feelings of hopelessness, inadequacy, and can make them feel worse and even push them deeper into depression.

If it were always possible for people feeling extremely depressed to pull themselves together and get on with their lives, there would be few people with depression. It's important to realize when people feel depressed for an extended period of time, they may no longer be *able* to pull their mood up by themselves. They need help!

There *are* ways to help the suicidal person realize his or her own life's value: *All involved need to seek help.*

Take Control and Fight for Life

If you are the one feeling depressed, listen to your feelings and the whisperings of the Spirit. *Seek help actively!* Ask for it. Don't be put off. Go to a doctor, a religious leader, a counselor. *Fight for life. Pray and pray again!* We are each responsible for our own happiness. Taking control of our thoughts, feelings, attitudes, and consequently our lives often means seeking out the best resources we can find to help us solve our particular problems. I have discovered that I must be a detective searching out ideas and resources to make life as full as I can for myself in caring for my mind, body, and spirit. I know that I must be aware of my moods and continually remind myself of my true purpose for living and of the true, lasting peace of mind to be found in right thinking.

I feel I must warn as many people as possible, any who will listen to what I discovered: *We are our own judges!* When we get to the Other Side too soon and realize what we gave up and the sorrow or pain we caused others, we may experience an emotional torture of our own making that is true agony.

The Great Benefits of Hanging On

There are times in life when you may be faced with the choice of giving up on life or going on. Please hear my message. *Life is worth living!*

Choosing otherwise can steal away great joys. It is not

a chance worth taking. I learned that life offers rich opportunities even in seeming defeats. Glorious rewards can be earned and enjoyed in this life, and *especially* on the Other Side, with right thoughts, actions, and kind deeds.

Life-Threatening Myths

Circumstances are constantly changing—often for the better. At least during earth life, we can still repent, find solutions, and grow wiser. *Death is so final.* Suicidal thoughts are false, futile attempts to escape from problems, rather than solve them. They short-circuit thinking and add to problems and feelings of depression. Suicidal thoughts always contain *life-threatening myths!*

Suicidal thoughts actually stopped me from finding solutions.

When I was on the Other Side, the anguish from my wrong actions created an unquenchable burning and searing of my conscience. It was agonizing to realize I had lost great rewards of happiness as a result of my choices when enduring and hanging on a little longer could have brought me the rewards of eternal victory with my family and loved ones.

I feel that it is important to again repeat that only God knows the full answers to questions regarding those who commit suicide and only He can administer a fair judgment and decide the degree of each person's accountability. However, even though individuals may feel depressed and miserable in life, they *may* feel enormously worse on the Other Side if they kill themselves.

One of God's Greatest Gifts

During my near-death experience, I learned that life is one of God's greatest gifts to each of us. To throw it away by committing suicide is possibly one of the worst acts one can commit—it is offensive and disrespectful to Him. Suicide is a tragedy for all concerned.

Also, I learned that when a person has sincerely tried to meet their challenges and it is their time to die, they can pass on to a welcoming home from those who love them on the Other Side and enjoy the fruits of their labors on earth. He or she can look forward to the harvest of good deeds and good attitudes by having endured well to the end. Such individuals will be met by heavenly family, friends, angels, and God with mutual rejoicing over earthly achievements.

Chapter 32

≈

Highlights from Heaven: an Overview

My experience was the most realistic event of my life. While I was on the Other Side all of my senses were expanded beyond anything possible in mortal life. By comparison, earth life is the dream world. Realism is only found on the Other Side.

Taking just one example, that of knowledge—never during earth life could my mind have grasped what it did there. It was as if I were drinking from some vast pool of forgotten wisdom. Information poured into me the instant I formulated a question. And much of what I knew over there seemed to come from within me, as if from a dormant pool that had suddenly become energized in this different sphere.

A Sphere of Love

It was a different sphere—one in which knowledge was readily available to the earnest seeker and one in which the concept of time is meaningless. The past, present, and future seemed accessible on demand. And the place was permeated with love—love that rises to emotional heights undreamed of in earthly terms.

A Great Retirement Fund in Heaven

Another Great Truth that I learned while I was on the Other Side is that enduring well while making it through problems during earth life will bring such great satisfaction and peace of mind over there that it defies description. It is like discovering that there is a *great retirement fund in heaven* which is built by overcoming problems during earth life with loving, forgiving, and charitable attitudes and actions. Such actions create heavenly rewards that include lasting, eternal peace and joy.

What I saw was not pleasant, and added to the realism of the experience. Those who had committed suicide, for example, I saw that they were pitifully distraught people who had somehow broken a premortal promise to make the most of their lives. Their agony of missed opportunity was clearly evident; I shared some of their feelings because I had willed myself to die.

Life's events, good and bad, were put into an eternal perspective that finally made sense to me. Never, with the dim earthly understanding I had before my experience, could I have fathomed the meaning and purposes of life as I did there. I came to understand that earthly life is a gift precious beyond belief.

Another Chance

My return to life was a wondrous, welcome reprieve. My choice to return was driven by my desire to remedy my approach to life and its problems. With my new understanding of what I could have been, life, with all of its trials and challenges, became an exciting adventure with almost limitless opportunities. If I successfully dealt with those opportunities, then a boundless future awaited me—an expansive future, in a marvelous, glorious sphere, limited only by my own thoughts and actions.

It is difficult to put into words what I saw and felt on the Other Side. The anguish, the peace, the light, the scenes, the sounds, the expanded feelings and increased knowledge were magnificent, yet familiar. It eventually struck me that everything there was as it ought to be, a considerably different and marvelously strange world, not a replica of earth-life's sphere.

Healing Defies Medical Wisdom

Other events after my return gave further evidence of the reality of my experience. The healing I enjoyed after my horribly debilitating illness, although not complete, was sufficient to allow me to realize my new-found life's mission. This healing defied most medical wisdom of the time. My recognition of the devastation created by my infected tooth was unexplainable by the best medical help I could get at the time. Yet the tooth's removal proved the efficacy of my Other Side's vision.

Fulfilling My Mission

My experience was the essence of reality. Purposely I believe, my memory has dimmed of some of the things I knew with such clarity on the Other Side, still the vision of that wondrous place is vivid in my mind. It will always be so. When flashes of memory bring back some of the feelings I felt there, I experience a longing or homesickness for what I know to be my real home. Fortunately, these feelings evolve into a desire to live this life to the fullest—to measure up to my full stature as a daughter of God. Someday, from the Other Side, I will look back at my actions in this life. Then I want to know that I lived up to my premortal promises and fulfilled my mission in life and my purpose for living.

The following are some of the most vivid impressions I received from my Other Side experience:

Sincere Givers Gain

As we give, so shall we receive:
When we give criticism,
we receive criticism.

When we are hostile,
we cause fighting.

When we ridicule,
we receive ridicule and
become shy.

When we are tolerant,
we learn to be patient.

When we give praise,
we learn to appreciate others and
we receive appreciation.

When we are fair,
we are more apt to receive
justice.

When we have faith,
we receive security.

When we give approval,
we receive love.

When we give friendship, acceptance, and
unconditional love, we find
peace and love in the world . . . Sincere Givers gain.

Joyce H. Brown

I pray that this book will be an influence for good to those who feel overwhelmed and stressed by life and to those who mistakenly long for the peace of death. I especially pray that it will restrain those who may be contemplating ending their own lives.

As I ponder and consider my experiences on the Other Side, my outstanding impressions are of the importance of being forgiving, of unconditionally loving others, and of not judging, criticizing, nor complaining.

Vividly, I remember the feelings of absolute, all-encompassing *LOVE* that radiated, permeated, and engulfed me. I personally learned that **GOD IS REAL!** During my near-death experience, I also learned **God's Heavenly Answers for Stress and Grief Relief Now**™ and *How to Make Certain to Enjoy the Other Side When We Get There.*

Afterword

Heavenly Stepping Stones

Several months after my experience on the Other Side in 1983, I met and married Earl Brown. I want to thank him and acknowledge his loving enthusiasm and encouragement for this book and its messages. I know his concern continues beyond the day of his accidental death in 1998 when he was called to return to God on the Other Side.

Since the book was first published in 1997, many additional things have happened in my life. In 1998 I became a widow when Earl died unexpectedly. The seven years following his death were difficult. I had the "growing experiences" of surviving severe accidents, health problems, the tragic death of my mother and eight other family members, and the loss of time and money from betrayal of false friends.

A Honeymoon and a Fire

Then I received a great, unexpected miracle. I met Ronald Runnells. We had a storybook courtship, romance, and marriage. However, while we were on our honeymoon, we were informed of a random act of arson. My home of 34 years, and everything in it, was totally burned including my laptop computer, which I was using to add current comments before I published the new edition of this book.

My insurance was inadequate to cover such a loss. This catastrophe, in addition to financial and health problems caused me grief that was challenging to overcome. In prayer, I felt heavenly whisperings that I would gain spiritually from this experience. However, my knowledge that problems are opportunities for mental and spiritual growth was severely tested.

Small Treasures Recovered and Lesson Learned

Day after day for several months, Ron and I dug through burned rubble hoping to salvage pictures, documents, and a few treasured mementos. Many times I quietly dried tears as I knelt in prayer and thanked God that my life had been spared. However, I could not let the debris be scooped up and hauled away until I looked through it all. Some of the pictures, notes, and correspondence that I found were priceless and worth the effort.

My famous gold-crowned tooth was found in the rubble, still intact, in the little brown prescription bottle where I had placed it years before. This became another great learning experience. My life since has been filled with miracles, insights, and loving relationships which became the heavenly stepping stones to the peace of mind and joy that I now have, which is more than I ever thought possible.

From My Heart to Yours: A Message of Hope

I have a heart-felt desire to make this book, *God's Heavenly Answers*, and its messages of hope and reasons for living available to those who are stressed, depressed, and/or suicidal. Personal knowledge has fueled my soul-felt desire to keep on keeping on sharing discovered eternal truths about the Other Side.

The Gold Crowned Tooth Was Found in the Rubble, 2006

I know that God is real. The Other Side is real. The God's Heavenly Answers I was shown during my near-death experience are eternal truths. Returning to life on earth was a miracle. Being shown the reason for my ill health was a miracle.

I know that making it through problems can make us stronger. And even though at times sad tears spill down my cheeks, with feelings of sincere gratitude, I thank God for countless, eternal blessings, including the many hard experiences which have strengthened me. And I know that it is not who or what is gone that counts, but who or what I have left and how I live my life that really matters.

My Desire to Spread This Message

There are many people who desperately need hope. They need to know that regardless of the difficulties in life, they can find the joy and peace I have now. Also in special need are people who have given up and need encouragement to keep living day-to-day after the loss of loved ones or experiencing other catastrophes.

With sincere prayers for God's loving mercy to ease my grief, pain, and sorrow, my feelings of devastation were swept away as I became even more determined to help others gain inspiration to keep on keeping on through their own challenges.

In spite of great financial losses, trials, tribulations, and calamities, miraculous events have occurred in my life. They have brought me more love, light, and enjoyment than I ever thought possible. I am truly blessed.

Letters From Readers

When I first wrote this book and published it in 1997, I didn't know what to expect or how it would be received. But as letters came in from readers, I felt overwhelmed by their comments and the life-changing experiences they told me about. I lost many of the letters in the fire that ravaged my home, but I did recover a few and wanted to share some of their comments here in this new and updated version of my book in the hopes that others will find their comments helpful as well.

~   ~   ~

Dear Dr. Joyce,

Thank you so very much for coming into my life. You are an Angel sent from GOD. I thank you for your energies and your love. You are truly an inspiration to me, and it filters down to those I encounter. For such a blessing as you, I give thanks. You have helped so many people along the way. Dr. Joyce, I just want you to know that your book has been a BLESSING in my life, and for that I am truly grateful. Thank you, and may God forever bless you.

Sincerely,

Ruby deBraux

Dear Joyce,

I have been suffering from severe bipolar and Post Traumatic Stress disorder for over 20 years. Countless times I have been lured by false hope that suicide would end my suffering. After several critical attempts and countless hospitalizations, I found your book. It was truly an answer to prayer!

God's Heavenly Answers contains life-saving facts for those contemplating suicide, and eternal truths that we ALL need in order to fully have the peace in the afterlife that we desire. I feel this book should be standard issue for everyone entering psychiatric treatment. If that were done, countless dollars, in-patient stays, and immeasurable human suffering could be eliminated. Also, this book is an invaluable tool for clergy of all faiths who so many times find themselves struggling to find effective counsel for those suffering in their congregations.

Your guidance regarding the urgency of proper use of time; the fact that we create our own heaven or hell, and the absolute necessity to take complete responsibility for our thoughts and actions are desperately needed messages in today's society. Truly, your book is a work of inspiration, capable of educating against many of the deadly misconceptions that haunt us, and giving our souls the necessary tools to reach for the greatest heights for which we were created.

Your book brings blessings to the reader on multiple levels. As I was reading about your life review, I found myself conducting a review of my own soul, and immediately identified shortcomings that I know could "bankrupt" me in the After Life. *God's Heavenly Answers* serves as a kind of After Life SAT exam: allowing us to find out if we have the "right stuff" to enter Heaven and have it be the nirvana we all want it to be.

Thank you so much for enduring the depths of darkness, and coming back to show us the path to that ultimate Light. I'm sure that because of this book, you will find your "Heavenly savings account" balance to be beyond your wildest dreams!

I will be indebted to you forever.
Love in Truth,
Betty M.

Dear Dr. Joyce,
I wanted to tell you about my friend who I used to work with. (I lost my job recently.) She has been struggling a lot through her life and relies on many depression and anxiety pills. I have been wanting her to read your book *God's Heavenly Answers* and I recently found the copy you gave me when you first wrote it. I knew it would help her in her life.

She lost her mom last year, a brother-in-law a couple of months ago, and her dog this week, who was like her child. She doesn't have any children and her dogs are her babies. She finally sat down to read your book this evening and she sent me a text telling me that she cannot express how much the book is touching her heart and speaking to her. She said it is exactly what she needed. She goes on to say that she is in awe and amazed and that it is the 3rd miracle she has experienced in her life. She said that God has answered her cries through the darkness by reading your book.

It has restored her faith and she is now crying tears of JOY. She says you are an amazing woman! Thank you for sharing your story. It is truly touching and does help those who are lost.
Love,
Kari Peterson

Dear Joyce,
Thank you for writing your book. I read and re-read it often in order to convince myself that life is worth living, no matter how painful or difficult it gets. I have many extremely painful health problems. In fact, I have been to the Other Side myself. I had become too "heav-

enly minded to be any earthly good" by wanting to be there instead of here.

After a series of tragedies causing me to lose almost everything, I didn't want to live anymore. Your book has helped me dramatically. It is such a strong and effective tool against suicide that I wrote letters and sent books to relatives, friends, and loved ones. I hope and pray your message will be spread by radio and TV interviews and even a movie.

Best wishes and thanks with all my heart.
Sheila Wall

I cannot adequately put into words how profoundly your book *God's Heavenly Answers* touched my heart! I am inspired by your words. Thank you for sharing your insight and experience with the world. Your book really touched me at a time I needed to hear your message. Please, please, please keep marketing it—it is needed.

Jan Snow, Marketing Manager,
PCS Multimedia Packaging

As a child, I was cruelly teased and harassed at school. I felt miserable and depressed. As a teenager, I foolishly quit school and got married trying to hurry and find happiness. Instead, my problems and unhappiness compounded. As a young adult, I was so depressed over my past mistakes, I seriously tried to commit suicide twice. In my late thirties I felt obsessed with wanting to die. I believed a perfect suicide would be the perfect ending to my tragic beginnings, and I entered into a suicide pact with my best friend. After reading your book my attitude changed. It opened my mind and my heart to life and to God. I cannot find words to tell you what's in my heart.

Thank you.
Suzan Walker

Reviews of *God's Heavenly Answers*

Dr. Joyce H. Brown is one of the most remarkable and inspiring people I have ever met. The previous editions of her book *God's Heavenly Answers for Earthly Challenges* have saved hundreds of people's lives who had been suicidal. We read her book describing how her "Near-Death Experience" reveals these answers in 1999, and were so deeply touched that we made contact with her and have been the best of friends ever since.

Joyce has helped countless people deal with grief and major stress issues in their lives. It is interesting, that more recently others have shown how almost all disease, which includes suicidal tendencies, are linked to stress. Society owes a great debt of gratitude to Dr. Brown for her pioneering work and continued contributions. How fortunate we are to have her book. It, undoubtedly, will be used countless times in helping people move through their challenges in life.

David W. Allan, Atomic Clock Scientist, Author of
It's About Time: Science Harmonizing with Religion

I have firsthand knowledge that the book *God's Heavenly Answers* is actually saving lives. The author, Joyce Brown, shatters the myth that all you have to do is kill yourself to get to a heavenly place of peace and beauty.

Joyce's near-death experience of being on the Other side convinced her that every day in this life is precious, that we can't win the prize if we take a shortcut and never finish the race, and that there is purpose to every life. Joyce was suicidal from the age of eight, and when her father committed suicide, she very nearly joined him. She often saw suicide as an option to escape the problems of this life, and consequently, often avoided the problem-solving process. Her experience on the Other Side changed her life forever and keeps her alive today. Her book should be read by every person who struggles with suicidal thoughts.

To those who are in a position to make a difference, I hope you will lend your influence and help correct some of the false ideas that are rampant in our country. Joyce's files are steadily filling with letters from people whose lives have been saved by reading her book. But she hasn't begun to reach the thousands who could still be saved.

Darla Isackson, author of *Finding Hope While Grieving Suicide*

God's Heavenly Answers conveys spiritual truths in a simple (but not simplistic) manner. Perhaps the outstanding feature of this book is not so much that it tells you entirely new revelations, but rather that which you feel inside that you have heard before, along with a spiritual sense of truth—a certain inspiration. Particularly recommended for those feeling depressed.

Stacy Harlan

A couple of years ago I was given Dr. Joyce Brown's book *God's Heavenly Answers* by a patient of mine who strongly recommended to me that I had to read it. Within a week I had finished the book and was on the phone with Joyce discussing not only the book but her interest in the connection between oral health and disease and the rest of the human body. Joyce had been instructed, while she was out of her body, that the cause of her illness was a specific tooth that was diseased and the bacteria inhabiting the dead tooth were releasing toxins that were killing her. As we compared notes from her perspective as a patient, and mine as a doctor, we discovered that we were on common ground.

Since then, Joyce has been a good friend and ally in support of good oral health both in preventing dental disease and in treating it. We also share an interest in the soul of humanity, the physical connection to the spiritual that is the essence of her first book and has been the focus of her life since her return from death. This cannot be better stated than Tielhard de Chardin's words: "We are not human beings having a spiritual experience; we are spiritual beings having a human experience."

Wendell Robertson, D.D.S., Biological Dentist

Pay It Forward

Keep the Message Going

The author, Dr. Joyce H. Brown, dedicates any profits from this book to help those suffering stress and depression, and to prevent violence, abuse, and suicide. Stress and Grief Relief, Inc., is a non-profit 501 (c) (3) public charity. Go to: www.StressandGriefRelief.org for more information or email the author: Joyce@hopedr.com. Offered are outreach programs that deal with today's most pressing emotionally based social needs for grief relief and anger management. There is a direct toll-free number for suicide prevention with counseling and proven life-saving material, and offer coordination and referrals to other agencies as needed. Donations are tax-deductible.

It is the author's goal and desire to make *Heavenly Answers* available to all who are in need of hearing its messages that God is Real, and How to Make Certain You Enjoy the Other Side When You Get There. What we do during our earth time determines our rewards on the Other Side. No matter what the problems are, peace and answers come from God.

Many people reported that they changed their minds about wanting to die after hearing about my experience on the Other Side, dispelling the myth of an unearned peace. Sharing my story as written in *God's Heavenly Answers* has proven to help people make it through their problems and rekindle their desire to live.

If you've received this book as a gift and enjoyed it, perhaps you can pass it on and keep the message going;

God is real and life is worth living. Books may be purchased at quantity discount prices.

Remember, NOW is not forever, but life is what happens while we are busy making other plans.

Suicide Consequences and Survivor Peace

Since my Other Side experience in 1983, I have discovered that many times, with the death of a loved one, or when a person in a family commits suicide, another person sometimes mistakenly believe that he or she can receive an unearned peace and instantly join the deceased person with a self-inflicted death as did three members of my family.

I know that *I cannot judge other people's actions* or the contributing circumstances that led them to kill themselves. However, my soul yearns to enlighten my family, friends, and others, who will listen, about the value of *making it through problems*, rather than quitting life because of them.

Whenever and wherever possible, I have shared my personal story and what could happen and the possible consequences of suicide.

Numerous people listened, and many of them responded to my message. I have received miraculous accounts and priceless personal stories from people who stated that they changed their definite plans to commit suicide when they heard my story and what they may face in the Afterlife. They, and many of their family members, have expressed gratitude for receiving a new Other Side perspective for living. They are helping share God's message to *"keep on keeping on,"* in spite of earthly challenges.

However, some people will not listen. After discussions with a close family member for 20 years, I received a phone call informing me that she gave up on life. She believed the myth that after taking her own life, she would automatically be swept away to some heavenly place of peace with God, not realizing that she could stand before Him, and be *held accountable for the pain she caused others.*

After her death, I believe in my heart that she had great remorse and anguish as she witnessed the shock, suffering, lasting hardship, and turmoil her suicide caused the family, and her friends.

For a while, I felt that perhaps I was to blame for her death because I couldn't talk her into wanting to live.

Finally, *in prayer*, I found a feeling of comfort. She had made her own choice. I realized that I couldn't take away anyone's free will, or whether they live or die.

The decision to reveal these personal family tragedies is shared as a warning to my readers that committing suicide may influence others to do so, too.

Even though *we cannot reap unearned rewards* on the Other Side, I want to emphasize and state that it is my belief that *only God can judge a person's actions* or determine the ultimate outcome. *Only God can answer our questions regarding those who commit suicide. However, with God's* grace and timing, survivors of those who have died or committed suicide can find peace and comfort to continue their own individual life's journey.

No matter the problem, *peace, comfort,* and *loving help* for problems *comes from God.*

Enjoy Life, This is Not a Dress Rehearsal

Look for, find, and create happiness.

Life is like a game. But the score is kept on the Other Side.

Giving up doesn't work. Earth time is limited.

It is worth finding out how to make certain you enjoy the Other Side when you get there.

As we give, so shall we receive.

Life demands that we must confront situations. Sometimes we have to change the situation. Other times we need to change ourselves.

Prayer, wisdom, and God's inspiration will help us to know the difference.

Enjoy life. This is not a dress rehearsal!

Just for Today

Just for today
I will be cheerful, loving and kind.

Just for today
I will try to adjust myself to what is;
Not try to adjust everything to my own desires.

Just for today
I will speak softly, be calm, patient, and forgiving.

Just for today
I will do a good turn or a kind deed.

Just for today
I will be as agreeable as I can.

Just for today
I will try to live through this day only.

Just for today
I will give myself at least a half hour for meditating,
counting my blessings and giving thanks for what I have.

Just for today
I will have faith, be confident and express gratitude.

Just for today
I will look for the good in everyone and everything.

Just for today
I will remember to breathe deeply and smile often.

*"Every adversity carries with it seeds of benefits—
The challenge is to 'keep on keeping on'
until we find the benefits."*

About the Author

Dr. Joyce H. Brown is an author, speaker, consultant, certified coach, and seminar leader. She is the founder and president of Grief Relief Now, Inc. a non-profit life-saving organization.

But Dr. Brown hasn't always been the dynamo dedicated to saving lives from suicide and depression. Even as a child she fought depression, so much so that she planned her suicide at the early age of eight. Her life continued to spiral downward through a series of tragedies and trials, including eight major surgeries. She ultimately became bedridden with rheumatoid arthritis and repeated episodes of pneumonia. In 1983 her physician told her to prepare for the end of her life.

Dr. Brown received the "bad" news with great joy. She was as ecstatic as someone else might have been if they had won an all-expense paid trip to Hawaii! She was going to experience her greatest desire … she died and went to the Other Side.

What she learned on the Other Side changed every perception she ever had about life and death, Heaven and Hell. She was taught the importance of giving MERCY, and NOT demanding JUSTICE. She learned that we have a great retirement fund in Heaven. We fund it when we make it through trials, do not give up, and we are loving, forgiving and do kind deeds.

Filled with regret for wasting so much of her limited time on Earth pleading to die, she begged to come back to her pain-wracked body. Finally, she was permitted to return to her earthly body, but with greatly enhanced knowledge. She was also shown the hidden cause of her illnesses that led to her death, and precisely what to do about it. She followed the revealed guidance and had a quick, miraculous recovery.

She experienced a dramatic revitalization of her life, physically, spiritually, and emotionally. She had discovered that suicide is NEVER the answer, but that life is precious, and our adversities are simply opportunities for personal growth with both earthly and eternal benefits. Most importantly, she learned that every person is a child of God with a purpose for living, and that we are ALL loved unconditionally by our Creator!

After her near-death experience in 1983, Dr. Brown continued her education in natural health and alternative medicine, becoming a Naturopath. She has received five life-time achievement awards in the natural health field. She is a Board-Certified Expert in Traumatic Stress for crisis management, a Certified Emotional Freedom Therapist, and a Master Certified Action Coach. She is known as the Therapist's therapist, AND the Hope Doctor!

As the founder and president of Stress and Grief Relief, Inc., she administers a suicide prevention hotline (800) 675-1777, reaching hundreds of potential suicide victims each year with a message of hope.

In addition to being the author of the book, "God's Heavenly Answers," an expanded and updated edition of "Heavenly Answers for Earthly challenges," Dr. Brown is the author of "Reap a Miracle Journal," "Manage Stress and Learn While You Sleep," and the Sleep-Learning CD, "Whispers for Life and Prosperity."

She shares unique methods about how to achieve *Stress and Grief Relief Now!*

Touching Messages
From Loved Ones

Love Notes that Have Kept Me Keeping On:

One of the joys of my life was receiving a note recently that said:

"We are who we are today because of you." It was signed by:

Lorena Novasio, Granddaughter
Jaiden Novasio, Great-granddaughter
Jesse Novasio, Great-grandson

Jaiden, my great-granddaughter wrote the following:

Light the Way
by
Jaiden Novasio

Brighter than a flame from a newly struck match, you
   shine.
You glow like a star amidst the darkness.
No matter where you are, you radiantly glow, an obvious
   sign.
You lead the way through the unknown, saying yes, anything is possible.
Without a leader, a strong delight, the world wouldn't be
   the same, a difference made by one soul, no fright to
   make an easier game.
One up on the bad, the evil doesn't stand a chance, you
   change lives, save lives, help when needed.
Most, you're pure light, insight, and amazing spirit in a
   willing host.
Intelligent beyond words, spoken from hidden depths of
   one's third eye, no wonder as to how we

Accept with open arms every word whispered softly with
no movement from one's mouth, the time is now.

Life is a gift, you help to wrap those gifts of ones lost
from a wrong turn, you keep the spirit alive,

Passing on knowledge of great inspiration and rare
knowing, lessening the hurt from the dark healing,

An open burn. A journey traveled by an amazing soul, it
hasn't always been easy, you've had troubles, just the
same as all,

A greater purpose, an experience so magnificent, pulled
you far the other way,

Saved you and made your true self . . . now YOU help
pull people up when they fall.

Logic versus Faith, you proved science wrong, you over-
powered reality and soon became very strong.

Your words of I WILL and I CAN filled your mouth
every day and you never gave up.

Prayer was important and changed your life, you gave
your all, put forth all you had through the pain and
hard times, you never gave up, only greatened your
stride.

Even now you overcome the impossible, there's no one
out there like you. I'm blessed to know you, let
alone be related as your grateful granddaughter, it's
true. I love you Grandma, I hope you know that I
think the world of you and everything you do.

Jaiden Novasio

Comment from my husband:

"Joyce, my wife, is the most giving, loving and forgiving
person I have ever known. Joyce's book *God's Heavenly Answers*
confirms the movie, *The Greatest Story Ever Told*, which was
about Christ. I feel that her book stands along with the greatest
books ever written because it is God's message."

Ronald Runnells

Author's Concluding Note

Reap a Miracle

I care. I want to share my message: That God is real and that we make certain we enjoy the other side when we get there by using Heavenly Stress and Grief Reducers. One of our biggest stress reducers can be using time wisely and lovingly, always keeping in mind our heavenly retirement account.

I want to share my message of the importance of our time and how we use it. It's almost like magic the miracles we can make happen as we use time wisely!

Time and how we use it is very important. I love the poem:

> *Yesterday is but a dream*
> *And tomorrow is only a vision*
> *But today well lived [making good use of time]*
> *Makes every yesterday a dream of happiness*
> *And every tomorrow a vision of hope.*

This world is not the real world. The Other Side is real and eternal.

I learned that money and how it is used here is like using play money. It is the intent of our hearts and what we do that add to our heavenly retirement account. Matthew 16:26 says, *"For what is a man profited, if he shall gain the whole world and lose his own soul? Or what shall a man give in exchange for his soul?"*

I sincerely care about people. I really care about our planet. I have a mission, I have a cause, I have a burning desire to inspire, motivate, and help people be all they can be, which in turn helps me be more of what I can be.

In my struggles for health, to live, to walk, to see, to succeed, I have had to overcome what seemed impossible obstacles by worldly standards. With the help of God, I slowly, painstakingly built the obstacles into stepping stones of understanding what this life is all about. I am trying to fulfill my real purpose in life, caring and sharing.

As I fought pain, paralysis, Rheumatoid Arthritis, Muscular Dystrophy, great financial losses, blindness, and loss of loved ones, I learned patience, tolerance and the real value of health, life and relationships. As I battled with Agoraphobia, despair, stress, and betrayals, I gained compassion, empathy and a love for mankind. I understand better, firsthand, what so many others are going through.

As I look back now, I can see that as I searched, struggled and pled for answers to my problems, I gained knowledge, wisdom, and information that can truly help many other people. I reaped miracles. We are all here to "learn the lessons of life." The ones I've learned have cost me dearly. I want to share them with all who want to learn. We need to care for our lives, we need to care for our planet. There are ways and means to live with a better quality of life.

My quest for answers has taken me to far corners of the world. I have literally gone to legendary "Holy Mountains" and to supposedly lost caves. I have worked with top scientists, world-recognized engineers, internationally acclaimed physicians. I have researched and explored modern and ancient manuscripts and have found some of the *greatest secrets of the ages!*

Yes, my life has been blessed with miracles, but I had to REAP them. I am known as a living miracle. I can teach others how to ***reap miracles too!*** Each of us can be more, have more, and do more for ourselves, others, and for this world. We can have a happier life, a cleaner environment. We can grow rich mentally and spiritually. We can have more time for fun, profit, and miraculous results.

I am only one person, but I am ONE! I can't do everything, but as I share my message with those who want to listen I can do SOMETHING! What I can do, with the help of God, I *will* do in helping make this world a better place for all of us to live.

I sincerely desire to succeed. My definition of success is the same as that given by Ralph Waldo Emerson:

SUCCESS

To laugh often and much; to win the respect of intelligent people and affection of children;

To earn the appreciation of honest critics and endure the betrayal of false friends;

To appreciate beauty, to find the best in others;

To leave the world a bit better, whether by a healthy child, a garden patch or a redeemed social condition;

To know even one life has breathed easier because you have lived.

This is to have succeeded.

REAP A MIRACLE!

Expect a miracle, believe in miracles.
BE a miracle for someone else!

Dear Readers

Depression is a very serious problem in our nation (and worldwide). Hopelessness is displayed rampantly, and suicides continue to plague our world. BUT, THERE IS HOPE!

Our organization is devoted to stopping suicides and overcoming depression. Every year, MANY people are given HOPE, and decide to begin really living! My book, *God's Heavenly Answers*, has proven to be the catalyst that brings true hope and change to many lives.

When adequate funds are available, we provide the book free of charge for those who need it, and to support groups and churches. Will you consider partnering with us to save lives?

If you have benefited from reading my book, I would greatly appreciate your reviews and recommendations on Facebook, Amazon, Kindle, Twitter and GoodReads.com, etc....AND if you have ideas on how we can better share the message of this book, please let us know. I'd also WELCOME your personal letters if you have found encouragement in this book.

The retail price of the book is $17.77. Quantity discounts are available. To order additional books, or to make a donation, please make your check payable to Stress and Grief Relief, Inc.

Stress and Grief Relief, Inc. is a 501(c)(3) nonprofit organization. Donations are tax-deductible.

As time permits, Dr. Joyce accepts speaking requests. If you would like to be notified when she may be in an area near you, please write to her or send an email with your name, location, and contact information.

Stress and Grief Relief, Inc.
450 Hillside Dr. #A224
Mesquite, NV, 89027

Questions or more information?

Need a book? Know someone who really needs a book?
Have a story to tell about how this book helped you or
a loved one?
Please write, call or email:

    1-800-675-1777
    Email: askwisdom@yahoo.com
    Website: StressandGriefRelief.org

15114508R00129

Made in the USA
San Bernardino, CA
16 September 2014